Magical Materials to Weave

Lotte Dalgaard

Magical Materials to Weave

Blending Traditional and Innovative Yarns

TRAFALGAR SQUARE
North Pomfret, Vermont

First published in the United States of America in 2012 by
Trafalgar Square Books
North Pomfret, Vermont 05053

Originally published in Denmark in 2007 by Forlaget FiberFeber

English translation © 2011 Ann Richards

ISBN: 978-1-57076-528-5
Library of Congress Control Number: 2011941725

Editor: Lisbeth Tolstrup, DJ
Project Assistant: Paulette Adam, FiberFeber
Technical Assistant for English Translation: Carol Huebscher Rhoades
Photos: Ole Akhøj
Illustrations: Christian Rasmussen 1.1, 3.2, 3.7, 3.10, 5.3, 5.4, 7.2, 7.3, 7.4, 7.5, 7.6, 7.8, 7.9
Drawings: Jens Bille
Graphic design and layout: Lars Pryds

Acknowledgements
Thanks to Grosserer L.F. Foghts Fond and Konsul George Jorck and wife Emma Jorcks Fond - without whose support this publication wouldn't have been possible.

Thanks to the models: Marie Svensson, Stine Oppfeldt and Ana Börjeson

Thanks to my colleagues here and abroad who endorsed/backed up my ideas and who graciously let me show examples of their work. Special thanks to Paulette Adam and my family who lovingly supported me through all the steps of this process.

Cover photo: A plisse scarf woven with flax and wool crepe and a rep selvedge with copper thread.

Printed in Singapore

10 9 8 7 6 5 4 3 2 1

Contents

1.1 – Lotte Dalgaard

Lotte Dalgaard and the Continuing Experiment

Foreword by Kirsten Nissen

With the publication of this book Lotte Dalgaard has begun a project that is not only praiseworthy and important, but also brave. The project is important because it concerns many topical subjects relating to textile craft and new materials, and also because it seems to me to draw attention to some of the movements currently taking place in design education.

Lotte Dalgaard is a skilled weaver with many years experience. In the new Millennium, as she herself relates, she has entered a new world, where the supply of different materials has given her a new platform from which to work. She calls them magical materials, and her curiosity, enthusiasm and perseverance shine out from every page of this book.

This new supply of different materials constitutes a unique situation in Denmark, and it is a situation that Lotte Dalgaard herself has been active in creating. She was a constructive collaborator in the preliminary work involved in setting up The Yarn Purchasing Association of 1998, and she has made a large contribution as a committee member of the Association, ever since it was established. The aim of The Yarn Purchasing Association is to supply members with a choice of yarns that are not available through the retail trade and so improve the base they have to work from, whether as textile artists, designers or committed amateurs.

The Association can now be said to be working well, with many members both at home and abroad, with a large choice of exciting yarns in stock. The Association's yarns are used in a multitude of contexts, as proved by the pictures in this book. Lotte Dalgaard has a zest for throwing herself into testing and using the yarns, partly in her work as a designer-craftsman and partly in her role as

an inspiring teacher. It is the fruits of this labor that we, as readers, harvest in this book. Another situation current in Denmark is that textile education has been undergoing substantial changes in recent years. The last remnants of the earlier, apprentice-based education have been irretrievably lost, the number of craft schools has been severely reduced, and professional design education has undergone a process of academization, at the same time as the concept of design has broadened. The approach of designing through close contact with materials is thus under pressure and it is therefore important, precisely at this point in time, that experienced practitioners should try to communicate their knowledge, recognizing that it now needs to be carried forward in a different way.

The exciting thing about this book is that Lotte Dalgaard aims to pass on her experience, both in terms of craftsmanship and experimentation, in book form. By doing so she contributes towards making some of the so-called "tacit knowledge" explicit. She normally conveys this knowledge in the form of movements and the spoken word, through personal contact in the workshop situation. But here she passes it on in the form of text and pictures. She not only provides good advice and practical experiences, but also sets out to communicate something as difficult as skill. Among other things, she describes the process of making a warp cross and concludes: "It is not so difficult, and it becomes like a reflex in the end. Just like cycling. Practice makes perfect!"

It is bravely done, since it is not an easy task to describe a bodily experience such as cycling, but I think she succeeds well in her aim. When I read her description of how a thread must be held at the right tension for winding bobbins, I can feel the imaginary thread between my fingers.

1.2—TITBIT creation produced in collaboration with the clothing designer Elisabeth Hagen. The fabric is woven in wool crepe, linen and turquoise copper thread and parts of it can be molded to shape because of the copper thread. It was shown at the Textile Printers and Weavers Exhibition "Stripes" at the Round Tower, Copenhagen in 2006.

Also, close contact with the material is Lotte Dalgaard's business. In many places in the book she goes in really close, and describes, in detail, the character of the textile materials, threads and textures, together with the handle and drape of the fabrics. This may seem to outsiders to be a rather narrow approach, but it is important to develop your ability to "read" these characteristics and effects, if one is to become expert in working experimentally with textile materials. Many skilled textile designers can testify to this, and proof in terms of good results can be seen, for example, in Lotte Dalgaard's own work.

Finally, in this book, Lotte Dalgaard is an example of what, in modern design research, has been called the reflective practitioner. Donald Schön, who initiated this concept, regards "designing as a conversation with the materials of a situation." According to Schön, the designer "shapes the situation, in accordance with his original appreciation of it, the situation "talks back," and he responds to the situation's back-talk. In a good process of design, this conversation with the situation is reflective."
Lotte Dalgaard works in this way regarding materials; considers them as active and magical, and having qualities such as energy, power and tractability. She invites us into an experimental situation where we can participate in this kind of interplay with the materials: "Throw yourself into it. Perhaps things will not turn out quite as you expect, but you can reflect on the result, consider it and use the experience in your next piece of work."

On behalf of the readers, I say: "Thanks for the invitation, Lotte."

Active and Stable Yarns— An Introduction

In this book I use the expressions active and stable yarns, and these terms require some explanation.

As far as I have been able to discover, there are no agreed terms or clear groupings of yarn properties that seem natural to use in this book. Overspun and elastic yarns, which contract in the finishing process, might perhaps be described as yarns that can be transformed. However, in a fundamental sense, all yarns are capable of transformation! One can, for example, transform a white yarn by dyeing it.

One can use chemicals to etch holes or cause shrinkage. Wool has felting qualities that alter its appearance. In industry, the terms stable and unstable yarns are used to refer to the degree of snarling twist. Highly overspun yarns are unstable. However, the term "unstable" has a negative ring to it and, to many ordinary weavers, will suggest a yarn that breaks or suffers from other weaknesses.

In her book, *"Ideas in Weaving,"* Ann Sutton refers to the activity and energy of overspun yarns. Similarly, during many years of teaching, I have used expressions such as active yarns, energy of yarns, power of yarns. In describing the different groups of yarns that I deal with in this book, my final choice has fallen on the expressions: active yarns and stable yarns.

Active yarns

Active yarns are those that, after a finishing treatment without the use of special chemicals, change their appearance, thickness or length. Active yarns have power, especially the power of contraction. One may talk of the "energy" of the yarn. In this connection one thinks of crepe yarns, elastic yarns, easily-fulled yarns, shrinking yarns and dissolvable yarns.

Active yarns include crepe yarns, which are overspun yarns with twists of 600-1200 turns per meter. These yarns can be either S- or Z-spun, and may also vary in thickness. Crepe yarns are produced from many different sorts of fiber—animal, vegetable and synthetic—and they can be single or plied. After weaving they are washed at 140° F/60° C, which causes them to crepe. The fabric becomes smaller and, at the same time, elastic—particularly if the crepe yarn is woven with skips on one or both sides of the fabric, i.e. floating over several threads.

Elastic yarns are those in wool, silk, linen, cotton or other fibers, that are spun or twisted together with a small percentage of lycra, which gives elasticity. The yarn may be plied with one or more threads, e.g. one thread of cotton with one of lycra. The easiest yarns to use are those where the elastic thread is twisted tightly together with the ground thread so that they won't separate. After weaving, where the yarn has been under tension, it should be put into hot water to achieve the maximum effect.

Wool suitable for fulling has properties that cause it to felt rapidly when washed in hot soapy water, an effect that is well known from the washing of pure wool sweaters and socks. In this book, such easily-fulled yarns are often used together with stable yarns, so that bubbly-textured or creped fabrics can be produced.

Shrinking yarns are those that shrink and become thicker in the finishing process, which results in their becoming inelastic.

Finally, I must refer to a special yarn, the dissolvable yarn made from polyvinyl alcohol, which dissolves in hot water during finishing, and so completely disappears. This yarn is used in one of the textiles shown in this book.

2.1—The textile artist Grethe Sørensen was the first in Denmark to use an overspun crepe yarn from Japan. Her pleated scarf has a silk warp. The weft is wool crepe and silk, which has been dyed with a gradation of color from gold to rust. Grethe Sørensen had seen the crepe yarn in 1991 at the School of Craft and Design in Oslo. In 1999 she visited the spinning mill in Japan and brought some of the yarn back to Denmark. It was immediately bought by the newly formed Yarn Purchasing Association of 1998, which Grethe Sørensen had been involved in setting up. The Association has made the yarn available to a wide public.

Stable Yarns

Stable yarns are those that do not change greatly during washing or other finishing treatments. Stable yarns include all the normal wool, linen and cotton yarns that we are familiar with, as experienced handweavers. Some wool yarns have undergone a special treatment so that they do not felt at all when washed in hot water and can therefore tolerate machine washing.

This treatment is a chemical process, which causes the scales on the wool fibers to lie flat against the surface, so that they cannot catch on one another and felt. These yarns are called superwash yarns.

Metal yarns also fall into the category of stable yarns. They can be made from many types of metal and are often spun together with various fibers. For example, a fine copper thread may be twisted together with one or more nylon threads, which are also colored, thus altering the color of the yarn as a whole. Copper threads coated with colored lacquer are also available in a range of colors and thicknesses. Gold and silver threads and stainless steel yarn are other examples of metal yarns that can be used to good effect.

Foil yarns, made from polyester twisted together with polyamide threads, are available in many colors and types and have been used in many of the samples and projects in this book. These include Corneta Transparent, reflective yarns and phosphorescent foil yarns, which are all stable yarns with very special properties.

New yarns are constantly coming on to the market, for example in polyurethane, polyamide and many other fibers. They have special properties and, while some are not particularly difficult to work with, others, e.g. monofilament, are much livelier to handle. There is just one piece of work in this book that uses monofilament for a pleated fabric (see Mette Kaa's dress, figure. 9.11).

In general, it can be said that many of the new active yarns work best when combined with stable yarns. It is the interplay between these types of yarn that gives rise to the many exciting and "magical" possibilities.

The Arrangement of the Book

"Magical Materials" is divided into several chapters: Crepe Yarns, Metal Yarns, Elastic Yarns, Practical Instructions for Working with Active Yarns, Suitable Weave Structures, About Experimenting—Weaving Samples, and Finishing of Active Yarns. There is also an appendix with technical information.

The first four chapters are about the different types of yarns, and consist partly of descriptions of the yarns and their properties and partly of suggestions for the easiest and most practical ways of working with them. Each chapter is illustrated with photographs of woven fabrics, and explanations of the effects and how they are created are given in the text and the photo captions. These chapters give tips and tricks to make it easier to achieve a successful result. Each chapter finishes with one or two projects, woven with the relevant yarns, and with basic instructions to encourage you to weave with the new yarns.

The sixth chapter gives practical instructions, providing a collection of ideas and information to help in working with active yarns, which are also often very fine. Some of this advice will also be found in the four chapters dealing with the different types of yarns, so, before you first get started, it is a good idea to read the chapters about yarns as well as the practical instructions.

I hope that the chapters on suitable weaves and on experimenting will be helpful when trying out some of the endless possibilities that are offered by these yarns. I challenge you to take the plunge into sample weaving, preferably working with others, for example, in your weaving guilds. It is exciting to create your own textiles, and that must begin on a small scale with samples. At the end of the book there is a glossary of technical terms.

If you are curious to find out more about exciting yarns with special properties, then look at the choice of yarns on the website of the Yarn Purchasing Association. (www.yarn.dk).

Crepe Yarns

Many of us, as children, have tied some leftover colored yarns to a door-handle, and then turned and turned and turned, until the yarns were so tightly twisted that, when folded double, they produced a nice cord. As we stood there twisting away, we were in reality producing overtwist.

Crepe yarns are overspun, that is to say, twisted so much that they form kinks or small crinkles. For example, the fine wool crepe from Japan has 1000 turns per meter. After spinning, the yarn is fixed by being steamed under tension, so that it will not kink and curl too much during weaving. Most crepe yarns seem a little hard because they have so many twists. If you wish to dye the yarn yourself, the fixing will be lost in the hot dyebath and the yarn will curl up and become unmanageable. Fortunately, many colored crepe yarns are now available through the Yarn Purchasing Association. In these yarns, the fibers have been dyed before spinning.

Everyone who has tried spinning knows what kinks are, that is to say, the small, overspun crinkles that form automatically when the yarn has too many turns. As a beginner spinner, one often holds on to the fibers for too long, so that too many twists run into the yarn and it contracts like a piece of elastic.

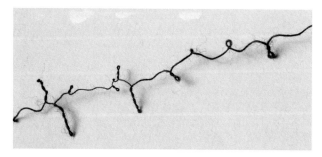

3.1—The overspun crepe thread forms kinks or crinkles.

There are substantial differences in the power of particular wool crepe yarns, even if their twist specifications are the same. It is disappointing if the weaving does not crepe as much as expected, and this can be avoided by testing the power of the yarn before setting up a large piece of work.

3.2—These three bunches of crepe yarn have the same specifications of 1000 tpm and 30/1. They are from the same spinning mill, but the differences in their capacity for contraction are obvious.

Just how large these differences can be is shown here, by the ways in which the grey-green, white and dark blue crepe yarns crinkle. This has an influence upon how good they are at drawing a fabric together and causing it to crepe or pleat. Therefore, it is important, when you first obtain a new active yarn to always test its energy. One way to test it is as follows:

Reel off a small hank, e.g. of 50 wraps, on a niddy-noddy, or a board if you do not have a niddy-noddy. Remove the yarn and rinse it thoroughly in hot water, according to the manufacturer's instructions. Dry the bundle in a towel and open it out with your fingers until it crepes. Always use the same board so that the hank will always have the same circumference. In this way a comparison can be made of how much the different yarns crinkle.

Number of Turns

A thin yarn needs to have more turns per meter than a thick yarn in order to be overtwisted and active, with sufficient power to form pleats in a piece of fabric. The number of turns per meter is given as Tpm = turns per meter.

An overview of all the yarns that are mentioned in this book, with yarn count, number of turns, fiber content etc. can be found at the end of the book, together with a list of suppliers.

There are many other yarns, available from various yarn suppliers, which are equally suitable. I have simply chosen to list certain active yarns with special properties, together with some stable yarns, which have been used for the textiles described and illustrated in this book.

S and Z Spin

Crepe yarns can be S- or Z-spun. S-spun yarn is twisted counterclockwise and Z-spun yarn is twisted clockwise. The fibers lie in line with the middle strokes of these two letters.

If the aim is to achieve a constant amount of contraction in a fabric, the direction of spin should be the same throughout a piece of work, but whether it is S or Z spin is of less importance. However, there are exciting possibilities for combining S- and Z-spun yarns.

The classic crepe fabric is woven with a stable yarn in the warp and an overspun weft, alternating two S and two Z spun yarns. The classic crepon fabric is woven with a stable warp and an overspun weft, which is entirely in one direction of twist.

See also the detail from Anna Nørgaard's reconstruction of an Etruscan cloak, which is woven with S and Z spun yarns, figure 3.8.

3.3—A scarf woven with a warp of 14/1 wool crepe with a dissolvable core. The weft consists of small stripes of lambwool singles yarn and 30/1 wool crepe. Most overspun yarns feel a little hard because of the large number of twists. The dissolvable core of polyvinyl alcohol is completely removed by hot water and this gives the warp yarn a completely different handle. The scarf becomes thick and soft through the combination of the three different yarns.

3.4—When the yarn is twisted to the right it is called Z-spun and when it is twisted to the left it is called S-spun.

3.5—This cloth has a warp of 30/1 wool crepe. For part of the warp, Z- and S-spun yarns alternate (bottom left hand corner), while part is woven entirely from Z-spun yarn (top right hand corner). The weft in this piece, one of my fabrics for TITBIT, is linen.

3.6—Z-spun wool crepe has been used for the warp and woven in 2/2 twill. At the top, Z-spun wool crepe has been used in the weft and this has produced lengthwise ribs. The lower part has been woven with S spun wool crepe in the weft and the most delicate spirals have been formed, because the yarns are spun in different directions.

When you have bought an overspun crepe yarn, check the direction of spin and mark it clearly as S or Z. Often this will be stated on the cone but, if not, you can check it for yourself. Take a length of yarn between your hands and try to twist it up in the direction in which you think it is spun. If it kinks violently, then you have the correct direction of twist, but if it twists up slowly and the fibers begin to separate, then you are twisting against the direction of spin.

▶**Tip:** With very fine yarns it can be extremely difficult to see the direction of spin. If this is the case, then try the reliable method I have illustrated.

Historical textiles with overspun yarns

Yarns that are very highly twisted have been used for many thousands of years. High twist yarns have mainly been used to make the textiles hardwearing, but also as a decorative element. In Denmark, overspun yarns were used in antiquity, again with the aim of making textiles more durable.

Anna Nørgaard, who works on reconstructions and copies of historical textiles, was approached by an Italian museum in 2003. The museum wanted a reconstruction of a cloak that was found near Verucchio, during the excava-

3.7—Pull off a length of yarn, fasten a piece of paper to one end and hold the yarn up until it begins to twist round. If the paper turns clockwise, the yarn is S-spun. If the paper turns counterclockwise, then the yarn is Z-spun. Once you have made this test, remember to mark the yarn S or Z.

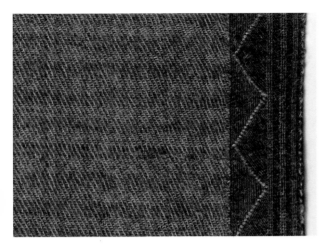

3.8—Cloth woven by Anna Nørgaard, using crepe yarn in 2/2 twill. Six threads of S yarn and six threads of Z yarn alternate in both warp and weft, giving a subtle checked pattern. Along the edge of the fabric is a tablet woven band, where the warp and weft threads from the red cloth are used as weft for the band. An incredibly fine piece of work.

tion of an Etruscan burial from 700 BC. Some well-preserved, neatly folded fragments of two cloaks were found in the grave of a man, together with weapons, jewellery and a throne that had belonged to a chieftain. Analyses of the yarn and weaving showed that the warp and weft were of fine, overspun yarn. This had been spun on a spindle so the amount of twist was slightly variable.

For the reconstruction Anna chose 30/1 crepe yarns from The Yarn Purchasing Association, the same yarns that have been used for many of the projects and samples in this book. She dyed the yarn with madder. The dyeing process caused the yarn to curl and crinkle—just as we saw when testing the crepe yarns—so she wound the wet yarn onto a reel to straighten it and left it there to dry. This fixed the yarn so that it was useable for weaving the cloak and the seven-meter long tablet woven band that forms the edge.

Weaving with crepe yarns

The crepe yarns first became available in Denmark through the Yarn Purchasing Association in 1998. The first piece of work that I made, using these new crepe yarns, had a warp of seven different types of yarn, in linen, hemp, ramie and wool, together with a single overspun crepe yarn in linen and ramie. The warp was made with the eight different threads randomly arranged in the warping paddle. I had an idea that the fabric would develop a lively surface with all these beautiful threads. I set the loom up for 2/2 twill, with 20 epi (8 epcm). On the whole, I think that these exciting yarns are shown to best advantage in simple structures.

It was a wonderful experience for me, when I wet finished the cloth. I never dreamt that the overspun yarn would have such a great effect on the whole structure of the textile. The slightly stiff linen and hemp threads lay in the most beautiful waves because the crepe threads contracted and became shorter. A delightful new world opened up before me, after 40 years as a weaver with everything tight and neat and in geometrical designs—always nicely pressed and with even edges. All this was completely overturned—it was wonderful to have a fresh starting point with these new yarns and the possibilities that they opened up.

When you weave with overspun yarns for the first time, they can be a bit troublesome. Many crepe yarns are very fine and can crinkle and break if you are not familiar with the many small tips and tricks that make the work easier.

Tips and tricks

Most people, unless they are complete beginners in weaving, will manage very well with a little practice. For yarns to be used in combination with the crepe yarns, I suggest choosing very fine yarns, since these allow the crepe yarns to work better.

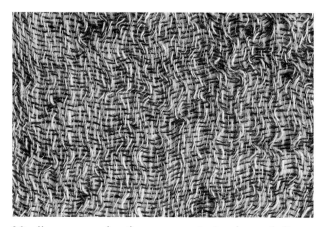

3.9—Here one can see how the crepe yarn contracts and causes the linen and ramie to form beautiful waves.

3.10—A thread wrapped around a smooth rod creates a little resistance for the right tension to prevent kinks forming in the warp or on the bobbin. A thick thread has been used here to make it easier to see.

Some good advice when working with fine yarns: take care to have good spectacles and a really good light!

When I am teaching I often meet students who sigh and say: "This is all too fine for my eyes." Possibly this is because many people who weave are also old enough to have grandchildren. It always helps when I fish out a pair of reading glasses from my pocket. And remember to have a good light on the threads exactly where you are working with them, either when threading the heddles or the reed. It is so annoying to discover, when the loom is set up, that there are two threads in a heddle or a reed dent, when there should only have been one!

Another piece of good advice: be patient, you are learning to handle something new that does not have the same feel as a thick 7/2 wool yarn such, and that cannot be pulled around as if it were yarn for making fishing nets. Those people who have woven with fine cotton yarns, e.g. 36/2, will be familiar with the rather careful grip, sensitive but firm, that is needed with these yarns. It is easiest to start by using crepe yarns in the weft, as a way to test them and their power of contraction. The first problem is how to make good and usable bobbins of yarn. Nothing is so irritating as bobbins where half the yarn falls off at either

end and wraps itself round the pin of the shuttle. And this is certainly no way to achieve a beautiful selvedge!

Winding bobbins with crepe yarn

The following section contains some good advice on the handling of overspun crepe yarns, together with a description of some of the possibilities offered by these yarns.

▶**Tip:** Take care that there is a little tension on the yarn before it reaches your fingers. For example, it works well to give the yarn an extra wrap around one or more rods on the spool rack. Small spools of yarn can be laid in a box on the floor, which puts a little resistance on the yarn. Without sufficient tension, small kinks (overtwists) will constantly form, which will run onto the bobbin. Keep a grip on the yarn, but not so firmly that the twists are pushed back along the thread, otherwise it will kink or break. Running the bobbin winder at a good steady speed also helps. The bobbins should not be made too big and the yarn should not be allowed to come too close to the ends. I lay the thread about ¾ inch (one and a half centimeters) from the ends of a paper quill, otherwise the yarn slips off and the whole thing becomes so tangled that it has to be thrown out. If you use

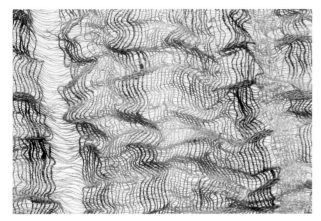

3.11—In this fabric I have used a new ramie yarn as weft, which is not yet available for sale. The warp is the same as that used for the project at the end of this chapter, with linen and crepe yarns alternating in stripes.

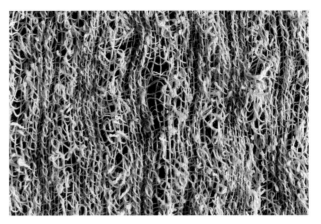

3.12—Between the turquoise warp stripes, there are open stripes, where the crepe yarn creeps out, creating a bouclé surface. I always try different weft yarns when I have a new combination on the loom. I keep these samples, since later on they may suddenly suggest an idea for something new.

wood or plastic bobbins with flanges then things are much easier. The majority of crepe yarns are supplied on cones, but in the case of the soft Merino wool crepe, which comes in hanks, a satisfactory tension can be achieved by winding the yarn directly from a swift.

▶**Tip:** In the absence of a spool rack, a flat board can be used to support spools. You can see a board like this in the chapter on practical instructions, where I use it for warping (figure 7.2). On another board, I have screwed a couple of handles on one side and some nice smooth pegs on the other side. This board can be fastened to a table with a couple of small clamps. There are then many possibilities for twisting a yarn once or more times around a handle, or up and down around several pegs, until it has the right tension for winding bobbins. It is also suitable for warping.

▶**Tip:** Some yarns are so lively that it can be helpful to put a piece of nylon stocking around the cone or ball of yarn. The two-ply wool crepe and silk crepe yarns are especially difficult to control. It can also help if you set the cone at a slight angle.

Crepe yarns as weft

The energy of the crepe yarn—the power of overtwist that is used to draw together the woven fabric—varies from yarn to yarn. This can often be judged from the tpm specification and, in addition, one can make a little energy test sample as described earlier. Also there is no harm in asking for advice from others who have already tried out the yarn. Many people are experimenting with these new yarns, and sharing knowledge and experience with others is very enjoyable.

The way the fabric is woven, the sett, combination of yarns, weave structure, number and length of floats etc. are absolutely decisive for the final effect of the completed textile. A warp made from a stable yarn with a relatively open sett, and woven in plain weave will give a crepe yarn good opportunities to work. The fabric will draw in to about half its width and the surface will develop a bouclé effect, because the crepe yarn's many small crinkles and loops are able to creep out.

If the same warp is set more closely, then the crepe yarn will force the fabric up and down, into small tight pleats or wrinkles. An even tighter sett, which almost gives a warp rib, will lock up the force of the crepe yarns so there is no appreciable effect on the surface of the fabric. These differ-

3.13—S- and Z-spun wool crepe is used to form different textures in the same fabric. Both warp and weft have varying setts.

3.14 and 3.15—Paulette Adam has woven a scarf with a wool/silk blend in the warp and 30/1 wool crepe in the weft. The sample shows the texture with weft setts of approximately 15 and 30 epi (6 and 12 ppcm). 30 epi has been chosen for the scarf, giving a fine, ridged texture.

ent effects can also be used in the same piece of work, for example by having open areas or by varying the sett across the surface of the fabric.

In the same way, the density of the weft has a great influence on the structure of the surface. Fabrics with the same warp sett—in a stable yarn—appear very different when woven with different weft densities. This applies both to a simple plain weave and to 2/2 twill.

Many of the instructions and pieces of advice given here should not be taken too rigidly. There are so many possibilities of slight changes in the thread count, sett, fiber quality and so on, which can influence the effect. So I urge you: see what others have done, and make some large samples, since fabrics contract differently in a large piece than in a 4 x 4 inch (10 x 10 cm) sample. Throw yourself into the work. Perhaps things may not turn out quite as you expected but you can reflect upon the result, consider it and use the experience you have gained in the next piece of weaving.

The two preceding examples showed how the fabric appears if crepe yarns are used for the whole of the weft, which is the simplest way to get started. But, when active crepe yarns are combined with stable yarns in both warp and weft, and used together with different weave struc-

tures, the possibilities become endless. I hope the guidelines that follow, together with the examples shown in the photographs, will be useful as an inspiration for your own samples and work.

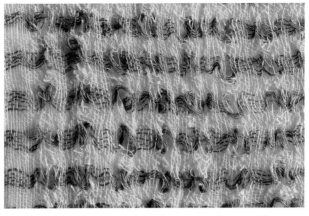

3.16—In this scarf the weft is 16/1 linen. This is equivalent to 11/1, 11,000 m/kg. This heavy linen bubbles up beautifully into definite loops. (More about the various systems of yarn counts can be found in other weaving books.)

3.17—On the same warp a very fine 26 linen yarn has been used for weft. The crepe yarn contracts more strongly than with the thicker linen and the fine yarn does not produce such large loops.

If you weave weft stripes which alternate between crepe yarn and stable yarn, then a brake will be put on the energy of the crepe yarn, and this will be greater if many threads of a stiff weft are used than if a soft fine yarn is used. An example can be seen in the samples of the bubble scarf, where there are empty dents left in the reed to form stripes (see figures 3.16. and 3.17). Here six threads of wool crepe alternate with six threads of linen in the weft.

Crepe yarns in the warp

There are many possibilities for bubbly and crinkled fabrics with a warp set up with stripes of a crepe yarn and a stable yarn, in a weave structure where the crepe yarn floats. Personally, I like combining crepe yarn with very fine linen. When the linen is pushed together by the crepe yarn, it creates a lovely crisp texture. The fabric can appear both glossy and matt, it is stiff and yet it crinkles and crepes, and these contrasts emphasize how each fiber has its own beauty.

With crepe yarns it is also possible to create many kinds of pleats and cords.

For lengthwise pleating and cords, a stable yarn can be used for warp, while a wool crepe can be combined with a stable yarn for weft. A warp that is not too closely set, in a weave structure with floats, will make the best use of the power of the crepe yarn.

To make crosswise pleats, the crepe yarn is used in the warp, perhaps together with stripes of a stable yarn. For the weft a stable yarn should be used e.g. in a simple plain weave (see figure 3.19).

I have done a lot of work using the Japanese 30/1 crepe wool as warp. The effect varies depending on the sett, as has already been described in connection with the use of crepe yarns as weft. This fine yarn is amazingly strong, due to the large number of turns per meter. The warp can be stretched very tightly during weaving. Too slack a warp gives problems with pulling in of the fabric and matting of the yarn around the shed sticks. A warp with approx. 30 epi (12 epcm) can be set up without problems, as was done for the pleated scarf project (p. 44). I have used the Japanese wool crepe at setts of up to approx. 60 epi (24 epcm) without great difficulties. Indeed I have even tried a sett as high as approx. 80 epi (32 epcm), though it was then necessary to use a skip draft.

When crepe yarns are combined with stable yarns, always take care to use a relatively open sett, so that the energy of the crepe yarn is not locked up. The closer the

3.18—This structure is given in figure 8.15, treadling 1, where the crepe yarn floats over and under 9 threads. Linen yarn in varying colors has been used in the warp to form the crests of the pleats. Fine wool is used for the plain weave picks. This fabric is woven on the same warp as the scarf and blouse shown at the end of this chapter.

3.19—These fabrics are of wool crepe and linen, with an edge of copper threads, and they become very sculptural when one twists and turns them. This gives many possibilities for use. There are instructions for the scarves at the end of the chapter on practical instructions (p. 44).

3.20—For these two samples I chose the weave structure shown in figure 8.15, with treadling 9 (above) and treadling 8 (below). This requires only 4 shafts. Crepe yarns are used for the floating picks, and the spacing of the cords can be varied by using different treadling sequences. Crepe yarns can form floats on both sides of a fabric, so that it is the same on both sides, or a structure can be used with floats only on one side, so that the fabric has two different sides.

yarn is set, and the more intersections in the structure, and the stiffer and thicker the yarns, the greater the resistance to the power of the active yarns.

If a checked effect is required, stripes can be woven that alternate between a crepe yarn and a stable yarn. This effect is used in the following project for scarves. In the chapter on suitable weaves, several ideas are given for such effects, together with guidance on working with crepe yarns.

3.21—The scarves shown opposite are woven in a check with active wool crepe and stable linen in a 2/2 twill. The same set-up is used for the blouse project that finishes this chapter. The fabric is very elastic and easy to work with and has a nice drape. The ends of the scarves are neatened with a small rolled hem and zigzagged on a sewing machine, before they are wet finished. See more about the sewing of pleated fabrics in the chapter on finishing treatments.

Blouse and Scarf

Bubble-texture fabric in linen and wool crepe for a blouse and scarf, which can be woven on the same warp. The blouse is designed by Elisabeth Hagen.

Warp: 30/1 wool crepe, 30,000 m/kg and 17/1 linen, 17,000 m/kg. Wool crepe colors: natural white, light grey, pale yellow, pale grey-green. Linen colors: 4 matching shades.

Weft: 30/1 wool crepe, 30,000 m/kg and 17/1 linen, 17,000 m/kg.

Sett: 20 epi, 2 ends/dent in a 10 dent/inch reed. (8 epcm, 2 ends/dent in a 40/10 cm reed.)

Selvedge: Ends doubled in heddles and reed for 4 heddles

Width in reed: 29½ inches (72 cm) Finished width approx. 18 inches (46 cm), but can be pulled out to the full width.

Total number of ends: 584 + 8 selvedge ends = 592

Weft sett: 20 ppi (8 ppcm)

Woven Length: The scarf is woven to a length of 94½ inches (2.4 m) and contracts to approx. 55 inches (1.4 m), though it can be stretched to a longer length. Weave the length you want, but reckon on approximately 40% contraction. The blouse is woven in two pieces of about 79 inches (2 m) each.

Warp length: For the projects given above, 7½ yards (7 m).

Weft sequence:

For the scarf: Alternate 8 picks natural white, 8 picks linen. Throw the shuttles for the two different yarn qualities alternately from the two sides. When the fabric is finished, the shifts from one yarn to another will make a good selvedge.

For the blouse: 8 picks of natural white, 8 picks of linen, repeated.

Weight of warp: 17/1 Linen, 4½ oz (125g) and 30/1 wool crepe, 2½ oz (70g). For both yarns, these weights are to be divided among the number of colors that are chosen. Here 4 colors of linen and 4 colors of wool have been used, i.e. 1⅛ oz (32g) of linen and ⅔ oz (18g) of wool crepe in each color.

Weight of weft: 17/1 Linen, 4 oz (110g) and 30/1 wool crepe, 2⅓ oz (65g) in all, for both the blouse and the scarf, divided between colors as required.

Weave structure: 2/2 twill.

Finishing treatment and making up:

The scarf is finished with a small rolled hem, before washing in hot water. See the chapter on finishing treatments. The blouse fabric is cut into two large pieces, which are finished in a similar way, with a small rolled hem, before washing in hot water.

▶Special tips for this set-up:

When yarns such as crepe and fine linen are used in the weft, the fabric tends to draw in, so the use of a stretcher or temple is recommended. The small marks that this leaves will eventually be completely lost during the finishing process. Any problems with broken ends can be minimised by sizing the warp with spray starch. (For more on sizing, see the chapter on practical instructions.)

Warp sequence:

30/1 Wool crepe natural white	4 selvedge ends	8								8 + 4 selvedge ends
17/18 Linen			8							
30/1 Wool crepe light gray				8						
17/18 Linen					8					
30/1 Wool crepe pale yellow						8				
17/18 Linen							8			
30/1 Wool crepe light gray/green								8		
17/18 Linen									8	
				64 ends x 9						

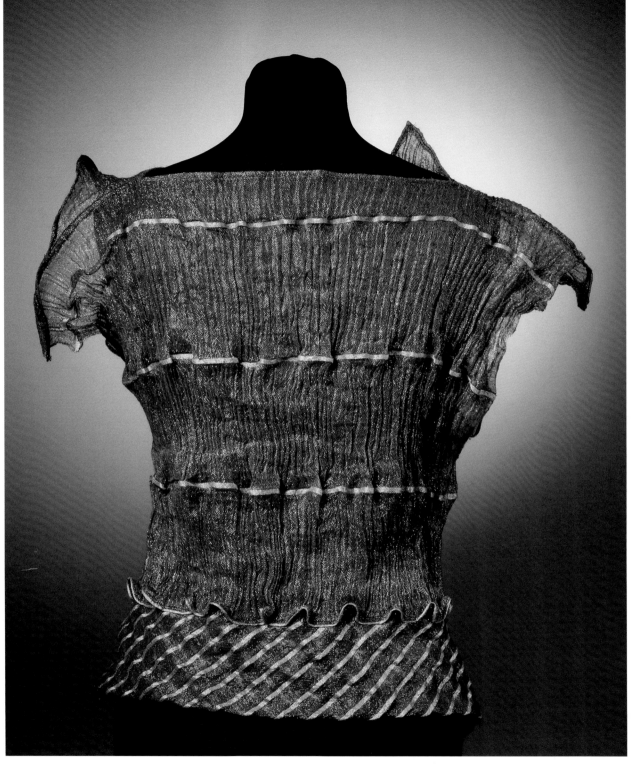

4.3—Blouse from the TITBIT collection. I weave the fabrics, while the clothing designer Elisabeth Hagen creates the one-off designs. The warp of this fabric is Corneta MX Transparent and the weft is a 30/1 wool crepe, with stripes of Jet Tex in a golden color. It can be clearly seen how the contraction of the active wool crepe causes the Jet Tex thread to form waves.

Metal Yarns

4.1—A fine copper thread, twisted together with two turquoise nylon threads, is used at the edge of this scarf made from linen and wool crepe. This gives an attractive edge, which can be shaped in many ways. Directions for making the scarf can be found at the end of the chapter on practical instructions (p. 44).

Metal yarns are available in many different qualities, both as pure metal and also twisted together with other fibers in various ways. Metal yarns vary a great deal, depending on how they are spun, how strong they are, whether they are very fine and whether they are spun together with another fiber. They are all stable yarns, which do not alter during finishing, although some metal yarns can be molded in the finished textile, in order to give it shape.

For example, the copper yarn, twisted together with colored nylon, which is available from The Yarn Purchasing Association, is one that I have used for the edges of the pleated scarf project on p. 44. It is a copper thread twisted together with red or turquoise polyamide thread. This yarn is fine, 30,000 m/kg, and pliable. Used in a ribbed selvedge, as in the pleated scarf on the cover of the book, it allows one to shape the edge by pulling it through the fingers, in the same way that can be done with some kinds of gift wrapping ribbon.

Pure copper thread with colored lacquer is available in thicknesses ranging from 0.1 mm–0.315 mm and in many attractive colors. These threads are very stiff and hardly suitable for clothing fabrics. Gold and silver threads may be made of real gold and silver, which are wrapped around another thread (called the core), e.g., of cotton. Gold thread is used for many church textiles. Often the metal is lacquered to prevent tarnishing.

The Yarn Purchasing Association sells very fine gold and silver threads, size 50, obtained from India, where they are used for saris. They consist of a silk core, which makes up 25% of the yarn, and 75% silver, since the gold thread is silver-gilt. These threads tarnish in a very special way, as can be seen on old Indian saris. Stainless steel is available as 4/2, that is, as a 2-ply yarn. It has a very beautiful grey color and a lovely soft sheen. It is used, among other things for bullet-proof vests.

Blends of metals and other fibers are also available e.g. linen and silk can be twisted together with steel or copper. These yarns are very fine and give a delicate, glimmering effect. Ann Richards, the English textile artist, has used silk/steel in her neckpieces and bracelets, where she creates pleats with sharp folds. She uses the yarn's ability to retain its form, when she moulds and shapes her sculptural textiles (see figure 9.12).

In this chapter, I would also like to mention the polyester foil yarns, which suggest an association with metal. These are made of polyester foil, which has been cut into very narrow strips and then twisted together with polyamide threads. They are available in many colors and types; they glimmer and shine, and are used as effect yarns in some of the samples and projects.

I have worked extensively with one of these yarns, Corneta MX Transparent, using it both as weft and as warp. It is a transparent polyester foil yarn twisted together with two polyamide threads. I have used it as warp for the black scarf with stripes of "gold" (figure 4.8). Also, in my fabrics for the TITBIT collection, by Elisabeth Hagen and myself, I have used this yarn, together with wool crepe in the weft, for several decorative one-off blouses, suitable for parties.

Corneta TM is made of black viscose, combined with

4.2—Corneta MX Transparent is used here as weft in a plain weave shawl with a warp of wool, linen and linen/ramie crepe yarn. I have used Corneta MX Transparent for scarves like this in both plain weave and 2/2 twill and have found large differences in the way that they crepe. With twill there can be a tendency for threads to protrude from the fabric.

4.5—This fabric, with Corneta in the warp and wool crepe and Jet Tex in the weft, has been used by Elisabeth Hagen to make fine textile bracelets, which are now are part of the TITBIT collection.

metallised polyester film. It is a beautiful yarn, available in both silver and copper colored versions and is easy to work with. I have used it in a relatively simple and easy set-up, together with a wool yarn that fulls easily, in a fabric for a little black jacket (figure 6.6).

Reflective yarns

Reflective and phosphorescent foil yarns are other stable yarns with special characteristics.

New yarns are being produced all the time, in polyure-thane, polyamide and other synthetic fibers, which have very specific properties. Some of these yarns are not especially difficult to work with while others, such as monofilament, have a livelier handle.

Lise Frølund, whose work is described and illustrated in the chapter on experimentation, has used reflective yarns to weave some attractive, small scarves, which are clearly visible in traffic (figure 9.2).

As all these yarns are stable, there are no great problems in working with them in the normal way. All the same, do take note of the advice that follows.

The size 30 copper yarn from The Yarn Purchasing Association is fine and lively to handle. For the edge of scarves and fabrics, I use it doubled in the heddles to form a tight rib, so that the edge will be firm enough to be shaped and hold its form.

Metal yarns have a tendency to slide down the cone and fall on to the floor. Annoying—for they are very expensive. It can be helpful to put a piece of nylon stocking around the cone.

If the copper yarn is used for weft, you may be unlucky and find that the copper threads cut through the warp yarn. This is particularly likely if you beat hard. So my

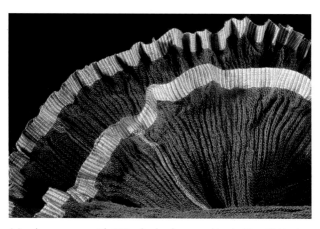

4.4—A copper yarn with 15% nylon has been combined with a silk/steel yarn to make a ⅜ inch (1 cm) wide ribbed selvedge to this fabric. The metal makes the edge so stiff that it can be pushed into different shapes. I have made sharp folds in one of the curves, while the other is stretched out, so that the small pleats in the fabric fan out. This is an effect used in many of the one-off TITBIT blouses.

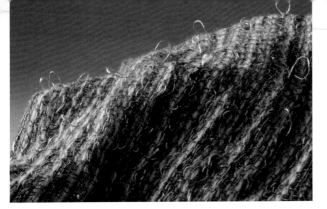

4.6—Here is a scarf that I wove with a rather open sett. The warp contains both ramie/linen crepe yarn and Jet Tex, together with various crepe yarns. This was not a great success! When the crepe yarn contracted in the finishing, the Jet Tex puffed up into large loops. A painful but valuable lesson.

4.7—This fabric has a warp entirely of Jet Tex and it is woven in a variation of an overshot weave, with linen/lycra in the weft. See the chapter on suitable weaves, for a jacket fabric woven on the same warp (figure 8.9).

advice is to use the copper yarn only in narrow stripes, until you have developed a feeling for how much the warp can tolerate.

I have woven many meters of fabric with Corneta MX Transparent as warp and the fine Japanese crepe as weft, and this creates a textile with a delicately creped appearance. The most awkward thing about Corneta is that it is difficult to see, because of its transparency and the way that it glints, so take care to set a light directly on the threads when threading the heddles and the reed. Take a break from time to time, because it is hard on the eyes.

I warp by taking the cross between my fingers (see Practical Instructions chapter) with only two threads at a time, otherwise there are big problems with moving the shed sticks back during weaving. As Corneta MX transparent is a foil yarn, plied together with two strands of polyamide threads, it can happen that one of the strands breaks and becomes pushed back along the yarn, forming a spiral behind the reed. This can interfere with other yarns so that they also break, and after that things can become quite desperate.

▶**Tip:** Starch is worth trying, though this will not always succeed in holding a broken strand in place. These yarns do not absorb the starch very well, so it may wear off. I have sometimes been successful by using just a touch of textile

or wood glue and rubbing the broken thread into place with my fingers. If you are careful and use only a little glue, this repair will hardly be visible.

The longer the length of fabric that one weaves on a warp of Corneta MX Transparent, the more strongly the fabric contracts into lengthwise pleats. If you then put in a stripe of a stable, slightly stiff yarn, the fabric will be thrown up into attractive waves. I have used this effect for a black scarf with golden stripes in Jet Tex (instructions on p. 28). Jet Tex is a filament yarn in polyester, which is also available in a silver-grey color. Take care, if you use Jet Tex as a weft on a very open warp, because it is likely to protrude from the fabric in large loops, which may not be exactly what you had planned.

If foil yarn is used for both warp and weft, then it will have a tendency to slip a little, particularly if it is used in a very open sett or a weave structure with few intersections.

If you are curious to know more about exciting yarns with special properties, then look at the choice of yarns on the website of The Yarn Purchasing Association (www.yarn.dk).

Scarf

Scarf in Corneta MX Transparent

Warp: Corneta MX Transparent, 86,000m/kg.

Weft: 30/1 wool crepe, black and Jet Tex golden 18,000m/kg for stripes.

Sett: 30 epi, dented 1-2-1-2 etc. in a 20 dent/inch reed (12 epcm, dented 1-2-1-2 etc. in 80/10 cm reed).

Width in reed: 28 inches (70 cm), finished width at the narrowest point 10 inches (25 cm).

Number of warp ends: 840 + 6 selvedge ends = 846.

Threading: 1 thread /heddle, selvedges 4 threads/heddle each side.

Weft sett: Wool crepe 30 ppi (12 ppcm), Jet Tex 28 ppi (11 ppcm)

Woven length: 69 inches (1.75 m).

Warp length: 2¾ yards (2.5 m)—so there is a little left over for sampling.

Weight of warp: 1 oz (25g).

Weight of weft: 1⅔ oz (47g) wool crepe and ¹/₇ oz (4g) Jet Tex golden.

Weave structure: Plain weave, preferably a straight threading on 4 shafts.

Finishing and making up:

After weaving, the scarf is finished with a zigzag stitch, before making a narrow rolled hem. See more on sewing tips in the chapter on finishing. The scarf should then be washed at 120° F/50° C, as Corneta cannot stand hotter water. The hem and the Jet Tex stripes give the scarf a wavy edge. The scarf should not be ironed, merely squeezed together. Corneta MX only stands a cool iron.

▶Special tips for this set-up:

As Corneta MX Transparent has no color, it is possible to make several very different scarves on the same warp. The more crepe yarn one uses, the more the fabric contracts and forms ridges. When stripes of a stiff yarn are woven in, the fabric forms waves. Try your own colors and stripe arrangements and create new variations. The two small samples are woven with stripes of 17/1 and 11/1 linen.

4.9

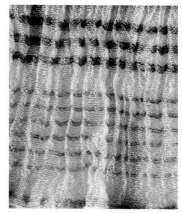
4.10

Weft sequence:

Wool crepe	1½" (4 cm)		8" (20 cm)		6" (15 cm)		6" (15 cm)		8" (20 cm)		½" (4 cm)
Jet Tex		8		8		5		8		8	
					(picks) x 10						

Elastic Yarns

Elastic yarns are active yarns, in which wool, silk, linen, cotton or other fibers are twisted together with elastic materials, usually made from polyurethane and called either elastane or lycra. We are all familiar with these materials from women's underwear and swimwear. They are very elastic and strong, though they can weaken after long use, which often happens with swimwear. When they are used to create structure and texture in handwoven textiles there is no such problem.

The properties of elastic yarns, and their powers of contraction, are entirely dependent on how large a percentage of lycra is included, and which fiber and method of spinning have been used for the accompanying thread. The easiest yarns to work with, especially in the warp, are those where the elastic thread is twisted tightly together with the ground thread, so that they tend not to separate. Yarns with lycra have been lightly fixed and, after being stretched during weaving, they contract when they are placed in hot water.

Take note that yarns containing lycra are very energetic, so not many threads may be needed to produce a good effect.

More details about the elastic yarns described in this chapter are given in the yarn and shrinkage charts at the end of the book. Unfortunately, some of these yarns are no longer produced, but The Yarn Purchasing Association still has some of them in stock and is working hard to source new elastic yarns.

Many people are inclined to group crepe yarns and elastic yarns together. This is wrong!

Look at figure 5.1 and note the completely different effects in this fabric. An ordinary wool yarn has been used for warp, and an elastic cotton yarn (bottom) and a wool

5.1—The difference between elastic yarn and wool crepe is shown very clearly here. At the top, the warp of stable yarn is woven with wool crepe, which creates small, lengthwise ridges. The bottom of the fabric is woven with cotton/lycra (colcolastic) and the fabric has pulled together without any particularly clear texture. The surface has a slightly bouclé effect and is very elastic.

crepe yarn (top) for the weft. It can be clearly seen how the elastic cotton/lycra yarn pulls in the fabric to half its width, but without any distinct structure to the surface. A slight bouclé effect is given to the surface and the fabric is very elastic. The crepe yarn, by contrast, creates very fine lengthwise pleats. (See more about pleating in the chapter on crepe yarns.) Both fabric qualities can be pulled out to their full width, but the sample with the elastic yarn will contract rapidly when the fabric is released. The cloth with the crepe yarn will, after some time, become a little more relaxed, and will need to be placed in hot water again in order to become nicely pleated.

If you make a test skein of elastic yarn and wet it out, using the same method as for testing the energy of crepe yarns, it crinkles up very tightly. The yarn has a massive

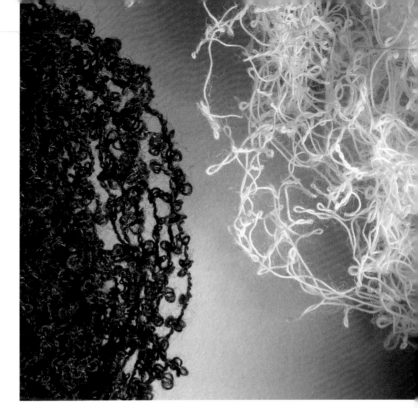

5.2—The different kinds of kinks/curls that develop in crepe yarns and elastic yarns after finishing can be seen here. The black yarn is an elastic 36/2 worsted yarn with lycra. The white yarn is 30/1 wool crepe, over-twisted with 1000 turns/m.

power of contraction. But it can be hard to judge just how much influence this energy will have on the cloth, so it is safest to weave a small sample. If you already have a warp on the loom, then use 4-8 inches (10-20 cm) of this to weave a couple of picks of elastic yarn, alternating with a couple of centimeters of a stable yarn. In this way you will gain experience of the yarn's properties.

Working with elastic yarns

There are no great problems in winding bobbins or warps with elastic yarns, as long as you remember to put a little resistance on the yarn, by giving it an extra wrap around a rod or something similar, while working with it (see figure 3.10). Very fine elastic yarn, such as silk/lycra, may contract so strongly that it can be difficult to find the end, if the spool has not been used for a while. Use a small piece of sticky tape to fasten the end of the yarn when it is not being used.

When you are making a warp, there should be just sufficient resistance on the elastic yarn that it does not curl or kink between your fingers, so take care that it is sufficiently stretched. Also, during beaming, it is important to hold the warp tight so that the elastic yarn is completely straight. The various elastic yarns perform differently so, for example, worsted yarn with lycra is easy to handle, both during setting up and weaving. In contrast, yarns such as fine silk/lycra, elastino (linen/lycra) and colcolastic (cotton with lycra twisted loosely around it) can be difficult to thread through both the heddles and the reed. It is hard to pull a single thread out of a bunch that is crinkling and matting together. The threads contract so much that they spring back when you let go of them, sometimes bouncing right back out of the heddle. This can be annoying when you are

trying to tie bunches of ends together after they have been threaded through the heddles, and it can be difficult to get all the threads into the knot. Do not make slip knots that are too small, with too few threads, or they will crinkle up and become difficult to undo.

Working with a warp of colcolastic requires extra care in setting up. Since the lycra and cotton threads are only loosely twisted together, the lycra thread has a tendency to spring right back as far as the cross-sticks and curl up there, while you are left with the cotton thread still in your hand.

▶**Tip:** To keep control of these lively threads, you can tie a cord to something firm, for example the cloth beam, or your leg, or around your waist. Fasten the threads firmly with a lark's head (the knot normally used for tying up the treadles), so that they are under tension (see figure 5.3). This makes it easier to pull a thread carefully out of the bunch.

It is useful to be able to control the ends after they have been threaded through the heddles and reed but before they

5.3—Carefully pull each thread out of the bunch, which is fastened with a cord around your waist. In this way the threads can be held straight and prevented from twisting together.

5.4—A small piece of cardboard with double-sided tape can be helpful in keeping control of the lively elastic threads.

are tied into bunches. Cut a small strip of cardboard and put double-sided sticky tape on both sides. This gives you a place to fasten each thread once it is through the eye of the heddle and, if necessary, you can also stick the cardboard strip to the bottom stick of the front shaft. Once the setting up is complete and the warp is tied to the front stick, the weaving itself does not present any great difficulties.

There are many possibilities for using elastic yarns to create effects in textiles. They can be used to create elasticity in specific places in the fabric, e.g. for clothing. Elastic yarns have such a strong power of contraction that it is easy to produce a bubbly effect by laying in stripes of two to four threads of worsted/lycra, in a fabric that is otherwise com-

pletely made up of stable yarns in plain weave or 2/2 twill.

The most exciting possibilities come from using the elastic yarns in structures with long floats, which can really exploit the energy of the yarns. Floats are produced when the warp or the weft does not bind closely into the fabric but forms a skip over or under several threads. As the floating elastic threads are not bound firmly into the fabric, their effect will be optimal. The material and the structure together create the texture of the fabric. You can read more about this in the chapter on suitable weaves.

5.5—A small detail, showing how elastic thread can be used in making clothing. You can decide for yourself how much the fabric is drawn in by the elastic, depending on how tight you wish this decorative area to be.

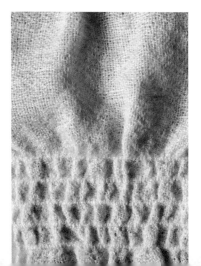

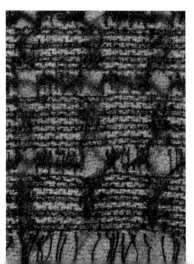

5.6—This fabric has floats of worsted/lycra on the wrong side of the fabric, in both warp and weft. The elastic thread creates raised squares. See the chapter on suitable weaves (figure 8.24).

5.8

Shawl or poncho

A large warm shawl or a lovely poncho. The fabric is a double-sided weave with two colors in the weft, so that the right and wrong sides are differently colored. This can be shown to advantage when the fabric is folded over like a collar. The weave requires 5 shafts and 8 treadles. It is woven in lambswool and worsted wool with lycra.

The shawl and poncho can be seen in figure 5.8 (previous page).

5.7—A detail of the wrong side of the dark red poncho (figure 5.8). Worsted/lycra, an elastic yarn, floats and pulls areas of the fabric together, creating ridges on the right side.

Warp: 11.3/1 lambswool, dark blue.
Weft: 11.3/1 lambswool, in dark blue, and worsted/lycra, in black, are used for both projects. In addition, for the shawl, lambswool in dark red, and, for the poncho, lambswool in turquoise green.
Sett: 16 epi, 2/dent in 8 dent/inch reed (6 epcm, 1 end/dent in 60/10 cm reed).
Selvedge: Doubled ends for two heddles.
Width in reed: 41¾ inches (106 cm). Finished width, in the smooth areas, approx. 38½ inches (98 cm) and, in the ridged areas, 27-29 inches (70-75 cm).
Number of ends: 636 + 4 selvedge ends = 640.
Weft sett: 30 ppi, 15 of each color (12 ppcm, 6 ppcm of each color). Where lycra threads are included, the sett should be 33 ppi (13 ppcm), so that the quality of the wool fabric remains the same throughout. Woven length: The shawl is woven to a length of 98 inches (2.5 m), finished length 79 inches (2m). For the poncho, two pieces 95 inches (2.4 m) long are woven, finished length 2 x 77 inches (2 x 1.95 m).
Warp length: 9 yards (8.3 m).

Weft sequence:
Shawl: Alternate picks of dark blue and dark red. The worsted/lycra is woven following the draft, where it is marked in blue.
Poncho: Alternate picks of dark blue and turquoise green wool, with worsted/lycra woven following the draft.
Shawl and Poncho: Start and finish with 8 inches (20 cm), treadling 1-6 using the two lambswool colors, i.e. without the elastic worsted/lycra yarn. Then following the draft.
Weight of warp: 1 lb 2 oz (510g) lambswool.
Weight of weft:
Shawl: 5¼ oz (150g) lambswool in each color + 1 oz (30g) black worsted/lycra.
Poncho: 10 oz (290g) lambswool in each color + 1 oz (25g) black worsted/lycra.
Weave structure: Double-sided weave with one warp and two wefts.

Finishing and making-up:
For both the shawl and the poncho, there should be 1½ inches (4 cm) of fringe at each end. The fringe should not be knotted. Instead, a narrow line of an open zigzag stitch should be sewn along the edge. The fabric

should be washed in a mild detergent suitable for wool. The lambswool yarn from Scotland contains spinning oil, so will need two washes in hand-hot water. The first wash loosens the spinning oil and the water becomes a little cloudy, while the elastic yarn will contract and the ridges will develop. With the next wash the fabric can be carefully squeezed until—if desired—a slightly felted effect is produced. The poncho is sewn together along the back for approx. 85 cm [34 inches].

▶**Special tips for this set-up:**
Using a stretcher is recommended, as the elastic yarn contracts during weaving and the singles wool cannot stand too much drawing in of the fabric. There are many possible color combinations with this lambswool from Scotland. The fabric is most attractive when one of the weft yarns is the same color as the warp. At one edge of the fabric there are no ridges, and so this part has been shown folded over to form a collar.

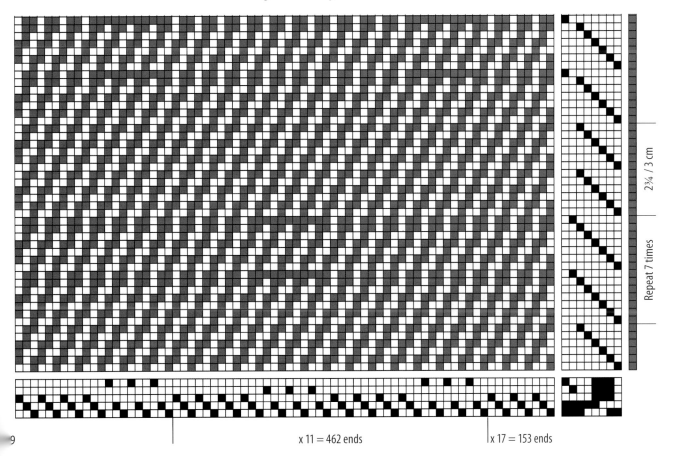

2¾ / 3 cm

Repeat 7 times

x 11 = 462 ends   x 17 = 153 ends

9

Easily-fulled yarns and shrinking yarns

These are active yarns that have some common characteristics in the way that they behave in the finishing process. They contract, becoming shorter, thicker and bulkier, sometimes also a little hairier, and they then become inelastic. When combined with stable yarns, a variety of lively textile surfaces can be created.

Easily-fulled yarns

Easily-fulled yarns are made from wool fibers which have good felting properties, i.e. they felt readily when washed in hot soapy water. The yarns are often spun from Merino, the type of wool that has the best felting properties.

Fulling is a well-known technique that has been used from the earliest times to give woolen textiles, both woven and knitted, a special finish and extra hardwearing qualities.

6.1— 28/2 Merino wool has good fulling properties. In some parts of this fabric the Merino has been threaded in the same heddles with Corneta MX, in silver. The warp has a very open sett. The fabric has been fulled by hand in order to have good control over the process.

Heavily fulled textiles become almost windproof and very warm. Well-known examples are vadmel, in the Danish folk costume, and the knitted pullovers worn by fishermen. Many weavers make plaids in woolen yarn, which are subsequently fulled and finally brushed to raise a nap.

The biodynamic, organic 28/2 and 48/2 worsted Merino yarns from The Yarn Purchasing Association are good examples of easily-fulled yarns. One of these is used in the fabric for the little black jacket with silver thread (project on p. 38).

Easily-fulled yarns do not need particular care in handling. They can be set up in the normal way, for example in stripes or checks together with superwash wool or another stable yarn. During finishing the easily-fulled yarn will felt, shrink, and become shorter, while the superwash yarn will bubble up.

The fine organic yarns, mentioned above, are only available in black and white. They can be dyed if you want other colors, but take care not to move this yarn too vigorously in the dyebath, otherwise it will become felted during the dyeing process.

6.2—This shawl is woven from superwash Merino wool, together with stripes of an easily-fulled, colored wool, from The Yarn Purchasing Association. These narrow stripes contract and gather the shawl into broad furrowed stripes. Woven in collaboration with Helle Hviid-Nielsen.

6.3—In this blue, plain weave fabric, checks of superwash wool alternate with the easily-fulled 28/2 wool from The Yarn Purchasing Association. The yarn was white and the fabric has been piece-dyed in Lanaset (also called Sabraset). Produced in collaboration with Helle Hviid-Nielsen.

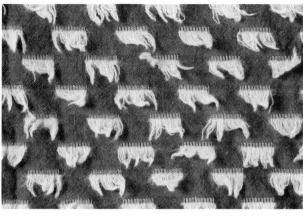

6.4—Detail of a silk shawl woven in a double weave, where the lengthwise floating threads have been cut after weaving. Finally the fabric has been fulled by hand. This shawl was made in a collaboration between Helle Hviid-Nielsen and the author.

Wool yarns with good fulling properties can also be used in weaves where they form floats. After weaving the floats can be cut and the fabric fulled. The cut threads will felt together in various ways, depending on the weave, the cutting, and how heavily the fabric is fulled.

More information about fulling is given in the chapter on finishing.

Shrinking Yarns

These yarns shrink and become thicker during finishing and also become inelastic. They are available in a variety of fibers, spun together with acrylic, which causes the yarn to shrink in water at 175° F/80° C. Polyester shrinking yarns are also available. Shrinking yarns can be used in the same way as easily-fulled yarns and will give the same effects. However, the fabric will not have the fluffy appearance that can be achieved with wool. Some of the weaving techniques, with warp or weft floats, which are mentioned in the chapter on crepe yarns, are also useful with shrinking yarns. Double weaves with a shrinking yarn in one layer and a stable yarn in the other, create lively, bubbly effects in the textile.

But remember, when using shrinking yarns or easily-fulled yarns, the finished fabric will be inelastic.

6.5—Double-woven fabric with a shrinking yarn of wool/acrylic in one layer and Jet Tex in the other. The finishing treatment causes the shrinking yarn to contract, so that the rectangles of Jet Tex bubble up.

Jacket in Easily-fulled Wool and Silver Thread

This quick-to-weave fabric is in plain weave with only 15 epi (6 epcm) in both warp and weft. The jacket was woven on a folding loom by Irene Madsen. Corneta silver thread creates a delicate silver effect during the fulling process.

Warp: Black Demeter 28/2 worsted yarn and Corneta TM silver/black size 30.

Weft: Black Demeter 28/2 worsted yarn.

Sett: 15 epi, 1/dent in a 15 reed or 1-2-1-2 etc in a 10 dent/inch reed (6 epcm, 1 end/dent in a 60/10 cm reed).

Width in reed: 32 inches (80 cm), finished width after fulling approx. 20 inches (52 cm).

Number of ends: 378 doubled ends (one black wool and one Corneta) + 102 ends of black wool. 480 ends total.

Weft Sett: 15 ppi (6 ppcm).

Woven length: 6 yards (5.4 m), finished length after fulling approx. 4¾ yards (4.35 m).

Warp length: 6¾ yards (6.2 m), so there is plenty for a small sample to be cut off to test the fulling process.

Warp sequence: 378 doubled threads, consisting of one worsted and one Corneta TM + 102 threads of worsted.

Weft sequence: Black worsted. Weight of warp: 8 oz (220g) worsted and 2½ oz (70g) Corneta TM.

Weight of weft: 6⅔ oz (190g) of worsted.

Weave structure: Plain weave.

Finishing and making up: The fabric is fulled by hand, so that the extent of the felting can be judged at all times. Irene did not hem the bottom edge but made use of the raw fulled edge. The narrow bands used for fastening have been cut from narrow strips of the fabric. Because of the felting they do not need to be hemmed.

▶**Special tips for this set-up:** Take care not too beat too firmly. The fabric needs to be very open, otherwise it will become too stiff after fulling.

6.6

Practical Instructions for Working with Active Yarns

Note: In this book I am using the European "back to front" method of beaming. The "front-to-back" method often used in the US is definitely not recommended for these difficult yarns. Before you begin your first warp of overspun crepe yarns, it is useful to gain a little experience and feeling for these yarns. When making a warp, just as with bobbin winding, the crepe yarn needs to pull against some resistance to prevent it running into your hands too quickly and forming kinks in the warp threads (see figure 3.10).

Making a Warp

The first warp that I made using the new yarns was wound with 8 threads in the warping paddle. Only one of these was a crepe yarn, but I found that, if I let this thread run directly from the cone up through the paddle, I got kinks in the warp. I quickly became good at pushing them to the back of the loom, so that the back beam became full of small kinks. But it was certainly irritating. The next time I made a warp, I managed to get the correct tension on the yarn by wrapping it around one or two rods on the spool rack, and the warp was entirely without kinks.

Since then, I have successfully made warps with up to 16 threads at once, with three of them being crepe yarns. To do this, you need to be confident about using a warping paddle. However, it is possible to get on very well without taking the trouble to learn how to warp with a paddle. As an alternative, I would strongly recommend that you learn to warp with two threads, using your fingers to make the cross.

If a cross is made with the fingers, so that the threads lie singly between the lease-sticks, this is not only a great help when working with active yarns, but saves a lot of time with all types of weaving. Warps made exclusively with crepe yarns must be made with two threads at the most,

7.1—This scarf is in the same type of fabric as my first work with crepe yarns in 2001. It is warped with eight threads of different linen yarns. One of them is an overspun yarn of linen and ramie. It can be clearly seen that this yarn contracted during finishing, causing all the other yarns to bend. I call this effect a wavy thread path, and it fascinates me very much.

and it is important that a cross is made between them. If there is not a cross and the threads lie in pairs between the lease-sticks, they will twist around one another and become matted together between the lease-sticks and the heddles, and many broken threads will result.

7.2—A holder on the floor for cones (an alternative to a spool rack) and a stick equipped with smooth pegs or handles, suspended from the ceiling, provide a good starting point for warping with lively yarns.

Making the cross with the fingers is done in the following way:

Set the two cones on the floor beneath the spool rack, and remember to give the threads the necessary tension. As an alternative to a spool rack, a stick fitted with eyelets and handles can be used to control tension, and may be either fastened to a table or hung from a doorframe or something similar. Take hold of the threads and keep your index finger between them at all times. In this way a cross is made between the index finger and the thumb, and this cross will be placed on the pegs at the top of the warping mill or board.

Make sure that the threads are laid down to create a singles cross so that, once the shed sticks have been inserted, individual threads can easily be picked up to thread the heddles. At the bottom of the warping mill or board, do not make a singles cross, but simply lay the threads in a normal cross so that they lie together in pairs. Take

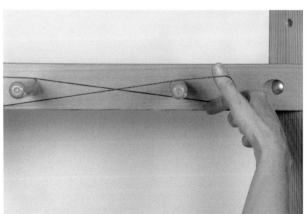
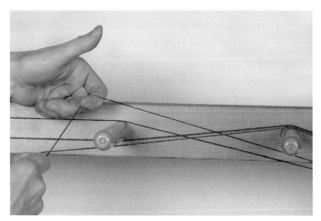

7.3 & 7.4—The position of the fingers during the making of the cross can be seen here. Also, read the instructions in the text. It is not that difficult and in the end it becomes a reflex, like cycling. Practice makes perfect!

7.5—Dividing up the warp makes beaming easier and more reliable— without broken threads.

care that the two threads do not twist around one another between your hands and the cones on the floor.

Beaming the Warp

If you want to set up a warp which alternates tightly set stripes and empty dents, it is best to distribute the threads by pre-reeding according to the overall number of epi (epcm), using a raddle or a coarse reed. This will ensure that the threads lie more evenly on the warp beam.

Before beaming, always divide up the warp by taking two dents worth of threads at a time from the raddle and carefully drawing them round the breast beam and knee beam. In this way you can separate the threads from each pair of dents from the rest of the warp and lay them tidily alongside one another (see figure 7.5). Beat and shake the warp during beaming with small rapid jerks.

When beaming a warp of wool crepe, elastic yarn or any other lively, delicate yarn, you should lay a round stick between the raddle groups, to clear any unevenness and separate any threads that are matted together or crossed.

Some people use two round sticks but for the crepe yarns I prefer to use just one stick, as it is then easier to keep control of the yarns. If you look at the picture and follow these instructions, with a little practice you should be able to beam a 20 yd (m) warp of fine crepe yarn without breaking a single thread.

With your fingers, lift up the contents of every alternate dent and lay the round stick between them. This round stick is supported by a pair of sticks that run from the back beam to the breast beam. The round stick is carefully worked forward to about the middle of the loom, so that there are no threads that are matted together or crossed. A section of warp is beamed on, and the stick is allowed to

7.6—Laying a round stick between the raddle groups is important when one is beaming fine, delicate yarns, and is a great help for warps made of crepe yarns.

7.7—Provided you do not have too many threads in your hand at one time, then it is possible to pull a thread backwards out of the bunch, even though, as you can see, they twist round one another.

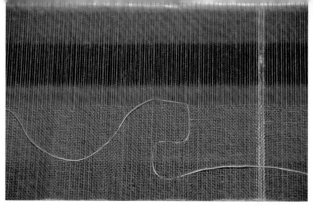

7.8—At regular intervals, measure the weft sett with the help of a counting thread. It is very irritating if there are more picks/inch/cm at one end of the cloth than the other, as the fabric will then crepe differently. A tendency to weave too tightly may develop so gradually that one does not notice, unless one is using a counting thread!

slowly move back until it is right up against the raddle.

The stick is then worked forward again, by lifting it or by making small seesaw movements, and any matted threads are sorted out. It is important that the stick should not, at any time, be pushed through the warp, because the delicate threads will easily break.

Take care to always hold the warp stretched so that the elastic or crepe yarn remains straight. If not kept under sufficient tension, it will easily crinkle and become matted and then threads will break.

I always lay paper in each round of the warp throughout beaming. Warp sticks are not so suitable for such delicate yarn. The slightest splinter will easily catch and damage a thread.

I use good strong paper throughout, but start with a very thick piece for the first round. Finally, a cord is tied around the warp beam on each side so the warp does not become loose during setting-up. Remember to remove these cords when you start weaving.

Threading and Reeding

When you are working with a small bunch of crepe threads that are twisting around one another, it can be difficult to get one thread out of the bunch without it becoming entangled. The fine crepe yarns can easily break if you pull too hard.

▶Tip: Take hold of the end of the bunch of threads and carefully pull the single thread backwards out of the bunch.

▶Tip: When you tie slip-knots with crepe yarns or elastic yarns, always tie them loosely and do not use too few threads. A small, tight slip-knot will curl up and become awkward to undo. If you make larger bunches of wool crepe, e.g. 30-40 threads, and use a loose knot, all will be well.

And finally: Always be meticulous in checking what you do when threading the heddles and reed. Find a system for checking that relates to the number of shafts, the threading repeat or the number of threads you take from each slip knot. When the yarn is rather delicate and difficult to handle it is best to avoid having to unpick the work and re-thread it!

Weaving

When working with fine, delicate yarns, it is better not to wind forward too much warp at once. Keep the fell of the cloth relatively close to the beater, and wind on only 4-6 inches (10-15 cm) at a time. This avoids the threads becoming worn due to the reed repeatedly moving back and forth over the same section of warp. The fine, inelastic singles linen yarns are particularly susceptible to wear from a closely set reed and they need extra care.

7.9 – It is always exciting to cut the fabric off the loom. By using this method, you'll avoid having to make a new tie-on.

▶**Tip:** If there are still problems with warp ends breaking (often this is worst at the selvedges), the warp can be sized in various ways to strengthen it. The easiest method is to use ironing starch, which should be sprayed onto the warp between the fell and the heddles. Push the reed back while you do this, and let the starch dry. This is easy to work with. You may find that you need to spray several times. The starch will be removed completely when the fabric is washed in hot water.

An older method was to spread a thin sizing of boiled linseeds over the warp, behind the heddles, using a wallpaper brush. Also wallpaper paste (without pesticides) is very effective. But both of these are rather laborious to work with and should not be necessary.

It is important not to allow the weaving to draw in too much at the selvedges. If crepe yarn is used for the whole of the weft you will find that the fabric very easily draws in at the edges. This is because the crepe yarn contracts, so it is necessary to use a stretcher. The marks made by the stretcher will be completely removed by the finishing process.

The lease-sticks should not be fastened to the back beam or tied together. When you wind on they should be allowed to move forward, and only when the warp has been re-tensioned should they be worked back carefully—one at a time.

Never move the lease-sticks on a slack warp, if it includes active crepe yarns or elastic threads.

It can be difficult to count the picks/inch/cm with these very fine yarns. If necessary, you can lay in a counting thread in a contrasting color. While you are weaving, count the number of picks there should be in 1¼ inches (3 cm) and check that these really do measure 1¼ inches (3 cm). It is more reliable to measure over more than ⅜ inch (1 cm) (see figure 7.8).

▶**Tip:** If it is necessary to cut off partway through a long warp, a lot of time can be saved in the following way: using a little waste yarn of a suitable thickness, weave a piece about 2½-5 inches (6-12 cm) long, depending on the openness of the fabric. Lay a stick in the shed and continue weaving for a couple of inches or centimeters. If it is a tightly woven fabric, this will be sufficient to allow the piece to be cut off without the weaving slipping. If it is an open fabric, then you can use wood or textile glue along the threads where you are going to cut. The fabric can then be cut off at the point where the weaving with the waste yarn begins (see figure 7.9).

You can now tie the cords from the apron or cloth beam around the stick and then you are ready to weave again. It is an advantage that the even tension on the warp that you have had up until now is not lost with this new tie-on.

Pleated Scarf in Linen and Wool Crepe with Ribbed Selvedge in Copper Thread

Here are instructions for the scarf illustrated on the front cover of the book.

There are many possibilities for color combinations with this scarf. It has alternating stripes of wool crepe and linen. The warp sequence given here suggests one possible arrangement of stripes. The scarves that are illustrated all have different stripes and colors, so you should choose for yourself the colors that suit you and are to your liking.

Warp: 30/1 wool crepe, 17/1 linen and size 30 copper.

Weft: 17/1 linen or another very fine linen.

Sett: Wool crepe 30 epi, dented 1-2-1-2 etc. in a 20 dent/inch reed (30 epi, dented 1-2-1-2 etc. in 80/10 cm reed). Linen 20 epi (8 epcm).

Selvedge: The 16 copper ends are threaded double in the heddle and 4 doubled threads/dent. The linen selvedge has three threads in the first two heddles.

Width at reed: 16¾ inches (42.5 cm).

Number of ends: 448.

Weft sett: 17/1 linen, 28 ppi (11 ppcm). Copper size 30, 50-60 ppi (20-24 ppcm).

Woven length: 2½ yards (2.3 m), finished length, relaxed, 39 inches (1m), which is a good length in use.

Warp length: 3⅓ yards (3m), so there is some spare for a small sample.

Weft sequence: The weft can be woven with 5-8 different colors, broken up by narrow stripes in contrasting colors. Look at the pictures for inspiration. Here and there, a stripe is woven in copper, with about 8 picks. Take care that you do not beat too hard, otherwise the copper thread may cut through the warp threads.

Weight of warp: Wool crepe 1 oz (30g), linen 1 oz (28g), if the number of threads suggested in the warp sequence is used. Copper approx. $1/10$ oz (2g).

Weight of weft: Linen 2⅓ oz (65g) for the whole scarf. A little bit of copper.

Weave structure: Plain weave threaded on 4 shafts.

Finishing and making up:
After weaving, sew a line of zig-zag stitching along the ends before making a narrow rolled hem. The scarf should be washed in hot water at a minimum of 140°F/60° C, and squeezed to help the formation of the crosswise pleats. Roll it up in a hand-towel and smooth it out flat to dry.

The scarf will stretch in use and become longer. It will contract again once it is put back into hot water.

▶**Special tips for this set-up:**
With these scarves, there is real scope for your own creativity with regard to color. The warp stripes are alternately wool crepe and linen. In the warp sequence given here, one possible arrangement is shown.

The weft has broad stripes combined with narrow contrast stripes.

In the chapter on crepe yarns, practical advice can be found on weaving with wool crepe.

Warp sequence:

Copper	16									
Wool crepe			96		88		52		48	
Linen		28		16		24		64		16

Suitable Weaves

Constructing suitable weaves is all about short and long floats and how they are combined. Many structures have been created in order to produce textured fabrics. A fundamental rule is that active yarns in a loosely woven fabric crepe a great deal, while in a closely woven fabric they crepe only a little.

There are many possibilities for exploiting the special properties of the new yarns by using them in different weave structures. In the chapter on active and stable yarns I refer to several groups of weaves and use various technical terms, such as floating threads, skip threading and double-sided twill.

This is not a book on weave structure, but in this chapter I have collected together some ideas to give practical help and inspiration, together with advice on which weave structures will give certain effects in the fabric, using active and stable yarns. Do not be nervous, even if your knowledge of weave structure is not yet very extensive. If necessary, you can consult the books on weave structure that I have recommended in the book list, where you can find further help with some of the most common weaves. Weave structures and drafting become fascinating when they are used to create special textile textures.

Computer drafting programs are very helpful, and many people are already making good use of them. It has become easier to experiment on the screen, print out, and then go to the loom with a draft. I have tried to give quite a few drafts that need only four or six shafts, because I know from my courses around the country that many weavers, working both at home and in weaving guilds or groups, have looms with that number of shafts. Of course, there are also ideas for structures on more shafts, including double weaves and block drafts.

For work with the magical yarns, I have divided my suggestions for weave structures into four groups, and this also applies to the photos of fabrics woven in some of these different structures:

1. Basic weaves
2. Crepe weaves
3. Float weaves
4. Double weaves

Note: All the weave drafts in this book are drawn with marks indicating sinking warp threads, because this is the most usual system for handweaving in Denmark and the other Scandinavian countries. That is to say, a marked square in the pattern draft indicates a weft thread passing over a warp thread. In industry the opposite notation is used, just as is the case with many books from outside Scandinavia. If you do not take note of this difference, you will have the wrong side facing you when you weave. It can be helpful to use a computer program such as WeavePoint, where changes innotation can quickly be made.

Where a thread is marked in blue on a draft, in either warp or weft, this indicates that it is an active yarn that will contract.

1. Basic Weaves

Plain weave, which is our simplest structure, is very useful for active yarns, both the crepe and elastic yarns. Plain weave is the firmest structure with the largest possible number of intersection points. The weft threads weave over-one-under-one throughout. Plain weave can give good creped and pleated effects both lengthwise and crosswise. Plain weave is, in fact, the structure I have used the most, for example, in all my fabrics for the TITBIT collection

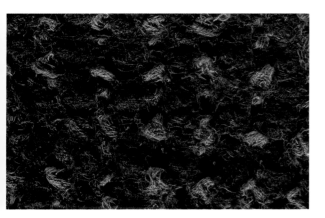

8.1— 17/1 singles linen, singles wool and wool crepe are used in a fabric with floats in both warp and weft. The crepe yarn forms the floats. With this structure, where about half of the weft is not bound into the selvedge, it is a good idea to leave an unthreaded end at each edge. This is known as a floating selvedge, since it neither rises nor sinks during treadling. The shuttle is laid in the shed over the floating end and will emerge under the floating end at the other side.

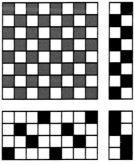

8.2—Weave diagram showing a skip draft.

that I produce with Elisabeth Hagen. I think that I shall never exhaust the possibilities offered by active yarns in a completely simple plain weave. Look at the pictures in this chapter and in the chapter on crepe yarns and see how greatly the warp or weft density can affect the appearance of the fabric.

It is best to thread on a straight draft (shafts 1,2,3,4, in order), since the treadles can then be tied up both for plain weave and for hopsack. A threading on four shafts can also be tied up for different variations of twill. However, if you wish to set the warp very closely, there can be an advantage in using a skip draft for plain weave, so there is the least possible resistance when the threads pass one another.

When basic weaves, such as plain weave, twill or satin, are used for the whole of a cloth, they give an even surface, an overall flat effect. If you wish to achieve a textured effect with basic weaves, then it is the various active and stable yarns and their energy, together with the closeness of the sett, which must be used to create that texture.

An example can be seen in the detail of Berthe Forch-hammer's scarf in wool, silk/steel and wool crepe (figure 8.3), where variations in the sett are solely responsible for

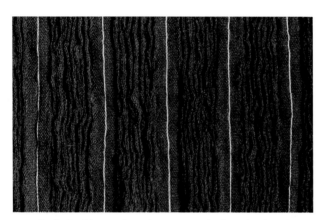

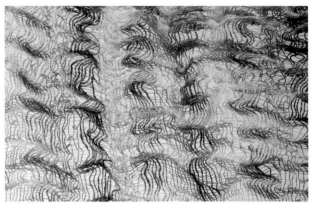

8.3—Berthe Forchhammer's scarf woven in wool, silk/steel and wool crepe, shows clearly how an open plain weave and a warp rib give entirely different effects in the lengthwise stripes.

8.4—A fabric with warp stripes of linen and wool crepe. The 2/2 twill gives the active yarn scope to work.

the different textures. The scarf is woven in plain weave. Another example is the bubble-texture fabric for the scarf and blouse in pale aqua (figures 3.21 and 3.22). The fabric is woven in 2/2 twill, with the same warp sett throughout. The bubbly effect develops because of small stripes in both warp and weft, which alternate between wool crepe and linen.

Using basic weaves, you can create patterns by using blocks with different characteristics. There can be combinations of different yarns, thick threads played off against fine threads, or active yarns against stable yarns. Or, there could be two different structures. For example, if a fabric has some blocks of plain weave and some blocks of twill, these will differ in the way that they contract and create textures.

The use of a single weave structure, such as 1/3 broken twill or satin, in blocks of warp and weft effect, gives a classic diaper effect. This is a structure described in most weaving books.

Lengthwise stripes of such warp and weft blocks will produce a very nice pleated effect, provided that the weft is either very fine, relative to the warp, or is an overspun crepe yarn. It is the difference between the diameter of the threads and also the pliability of the weft, that are important for the fabric's ability to pleat. (Yarn diameter is not the same as the yardage (meterage) of the yarn.)

In industry, the Ashenhurst formula is used to calculate the diameter of the threads, but this is perhaps a little technical for many weavers. In the chapter on experimentation, a method is given for determining suitable setts.

In order for the join between the two structures to be sharp it is necessary to make a clean transition between

8.5—An early piece by Ann Richards, using warp and weft effects with two different structures. For many years Ann Richards has worked with and taught about active and stable yarns.

them, i.e. no weft threads should float over the boundary between the two structures. Here in Denmark, some of the first pictures that we saw of this effect, using overspun yarn in the weft, were of work by the English textile artist Ann Richards, published in the American magazine *Handwoven* in 1996. She has worked in the most elegant way with the interplay between active and stable yarns (See also figure 9.12).

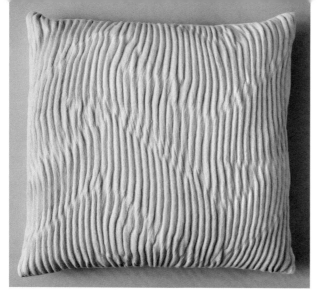

8.6—Karina Nielsen Rios, a young Danish textile artist, has used a satin weave with warp and weft effect. The fabric for the cushion is woven on a Jacquard loom, which makes it possible to create the organic form of the pattern, while the relief effect is created from the two weave structures, combined with a crepe yarn in the weft.

8.7—This fabric is woven in a variation of a crepe weave. The warp is 28/2 Merino wool, together with linen/lycra for the floating ends. The weft is a white silk/ramie from The Yarn Purchasing Association, with black 30/1 wool crepe, used double, for the floating picks. The fabric contracts considerably in the warp direction (approx. 50%) due to the effect of the linen/lycra. Widthwise, it contracts much less (approx. 20%) because the wool crepe is not as powerful as the linen/lycra. The pattern of small dashes is created by short weft floats of black crepe yarn, which are marked in blue on the draft. I have achieved a quality that is as elastic as knitting and, at the same time, produced a fabric with plenty of body.

2. Crepe Weaves

Crepe weaves are characterized by an uneven surface, formed from a mixture of short and long floats, superimposed on a basic weave. The structure is extensively used in industry for clothing fabrics. It gives an elastic cloth quality, which can be enhanced by using active yarns for the floats. (See the chapter on crepe yarns for information about crepes and crepons.) These fabrics are often woven in a crepe weave, and if you want a clothing fabric that is elastic, adaptable, with a good drape and no definite textural lines, it is a good idea to have a look at crepe weaves, and try them out with active and stable yarns. The larger the quantity of active threads that are in the weave repeat, the more the fabric will contract. For this type of clothing fabric, the sett should be relatively close, similar to plain weave or just slightly more open.

Like all other weave structures, crepe weaves can be endlessly varied by means of materials and sett.

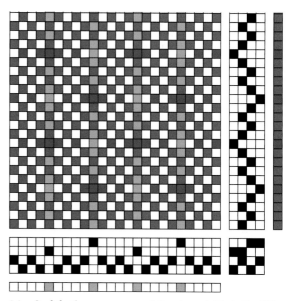

8.8—Draft for the crepe weave variation shown in illustration 8.7.

8.9—Silver fabric for an evening jacket, woven by Tonni Juhl Christensen in a variation of an overshot weave, which is described below. Jet Tex and silk/lycra have been used for this fabric, which has an oblique texture and is very elastic.

3. Float Weaves

With these structures, everything depends upon short and long floats and how they are combined, especially when we work with active yarns.

A basic rule is that, when the floating threads are not tied down by crosswise threads, then the power of contraction of the active yarns will be optimal, and the fabric will shape itself according to the number, length and position of the floats. The weaves that I am grouping together as float weaves include many that are well-known, such as waffle weave, cords, honeycomb, overshot, huckaback etc. These weaves are excellent for forming a textured surface, which can be ridged, holey, pleated etc. both lengthwise and widthwise, even when woven in a stable yarn. The strongest effects are produced when an active yarn is used for the floats. Many people will be familiar with the hollows formed by honeycomb and waffle weave, from their experiences weaving with normal stable yarns. Many of these structures can be woven on only six shafts and they can be set off particularly well by combining them with areas of smooth plain weave.

The draft shown in figure 8.10 is a variant of an overshot weave, a structure that is well known from classic Swedish textiles. I was fascinated by the way that the overshot weave can have 4 blocks on only 4 shafts, though I wanted to use the structure in a new way.

I therefore changed the tie-up, which in normal overshot is a plain weave tie-up combined with 2/2 twill. My tie-up consists of plain weave combined with 1/3 twill. The threading is the usual overshot threading with 4 blocks on 4 shafts. The longer floats of the 1/3 twill are exploited by using an active yarn in the weft.

The ground weft in plain weave can be a stable yarn

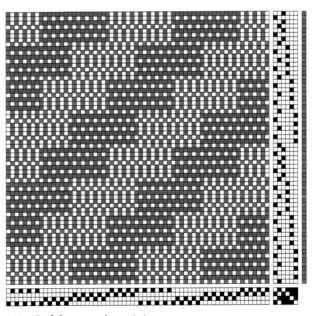

8.10—Draft for an overshot variation.

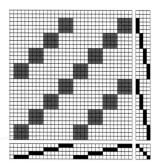

8.11—Block pattern with diagonal lines for the Jet Tex fabric.

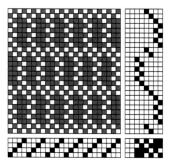

8.12—Draft for a weft-ways cord (pique).

or an active yarn, depending on how elastic you want the finished fabric to be. There is an advantage in weaving the fabric with the long floats uppermost, so you can clearly see the pattern.

▶**Tip:** This applies to all structures that have many long floats. Always tie up the loom so that the floats lie on the upper face of the cloth while you are weaving, even if you intend them to be on the wrong side of the fabric when it is in use. This gives a firm layer of threads for the shuttle to run upon.

I have designed the block draft (figure 8.11) for this fabric with a simple oblique line. There is inspiration to be found by looking at block patterns in books and magazines, but take just a single part of the pattern and enlarge or repeat it. Large, complex overshot patterns, with many small

rosettes and wavy lines, will lose their precision or become completely lost, when woven with active yarns.

▶**Tip:** If you are using two shuttles, with different materials, and are alternating between plain picks and pattern picks, insert the shuttle for the plain weave from the right hand side when you depress the right hand treadle, and from the left hand side when you depress the left hand treadle. Then you are never in doubt about which of the plain weave treadles you are using.

Pique weave (see figure 8.12) is also suitable for producing a ridged texture. A weftwise cord (pique) can be woven on 4 shafts, while a warpwise cord requires 6 shafts. One can play with different active yarns for the floats, while the ridges can be made more prominent and have different heights, depending on the length of the floats. One can

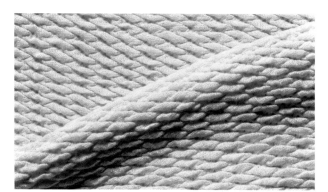

8.13—Karina Nielsen Rios has used a variation of a pique weave, in silk and linen/lycra. The fabric has been woven on a computer-controlled loom.

8.14—The wrong side of the fabric showing the floats in linen/lycra, an elastic thread that causes the fabric to puff up and form small raised slanting "arrows."

also produce cord ridges on both sides of the cloth to form sharper, zigzag pleating.

I have really enjoyed making different weave drafts using floats to create pleats and cords. The floats can lie on both sides of the cloth or only on one side, depending on whether you want a fabric that is the same on both sides or that has a right and a wrong side.

The draft given here contains many different possibilities for the tie-up and treadling. Let us take a look at some examples of different fabrics. In the chapter on crepe yarns, a variation of pleating is shown (figure 3.18), which is based on treadling sequence 1. The fabrics with small cords (figure 3.20) are produced by using treadling 2.

In the chapter on finishing, under the section on felting, there is an example of a fabric with "tufts" (figure 10.2). This effect is achieved by using treadling 8, and then felting the finished fabric.

Finally, take a look at the fabrics for the large woolen shawl (figure 5.8), the turquoise summer blouse (figures 8.30—8.33) and the small sample with black and white cords (figure 8.16). All these different fabrics were woven with treadling 5. All of the fabrics mentioned above have been made with the draft in figure 15 as a starting point.

I constructed this weave draft in connection with the many courses that I have given on the topic of the new yarns, and we have tried many of these different treadlings. The threading is on 4 shafts (so it can be set up on a small folding loom, such as may be found in the workshops of many weavers guilds and groups).

The tie-up can be altered, depending on which part of the draft you wish to weave. It does not take long to change a tie-up since there are, perhaps, only 4-6 knots that need to be changed, and you can then weave an entirely new

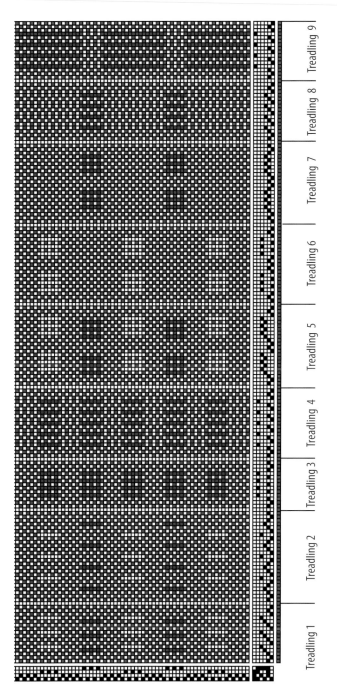

8.15—Weave draft with treadlings for pleats, cords and "blips."

Treadling 9 | Treadling 8 | Treadling 7 | Treadling 6 | Treadling 5 | Treadling 4 | Treadling 3 | Treadling 2 | Treadling 1

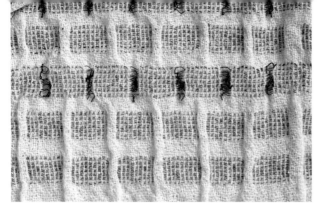

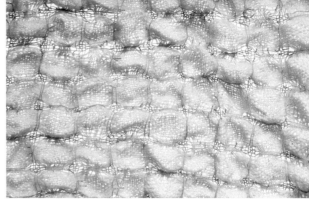

8.16—Here I have woven a sample, where there are narrow cords on both sides of the fabric. The floating yarn is black crepe on a warp of white wool. There are many possibilities for building up your own "brick" patterns by varying the treadling.

8.18—Here the floating threads form small squares, before weaving together in plain weave. With crepe yarns for the floats and a rather open sett, the cloth becomes transparent and the active yarn causes the fabric to bubble. The structure can be varied with squares of different sizes. Take care not to make the floating threads so long that they can catch and be pulled out.

fabric! If you have a loom with 6 treadles, then the whole tie-up can be set up in one go. Also, if you weave on a computer loom or direct tie-up loom, many different possibilities can be tried relatively quickly.

Depending on the yarn quality and the sett, you can decide for yourself the length of the floats and the distance between them. In a pleated fabric the active threads float on both sides of the cloth. Stripes can be arranged so that different colors appear on the two sides when the pleating pulls the fabric together. A contrasting color can be put at the top of a pleat, or colors can be placed so that each side of a sharp pleat has a different color. See, for example,

Mette Kaa's black and white dress (figure 9.11).

By studying weave theory one can learn about many classic weaves and their construction. This obviously gives a good overview, but you can certainly go ahead and experiment with structures such as floating threads, without being knowledgeable about such things. WeavePoint and other computer weave programs make it easy to experiment with long floating threads in a plain weave or twill ground.

If you look closely at the structures shown here in this chapter, hopefully you will be inspired to produce other combinations using floating threads. Sometimes it can be a little difficult to predict how the fabric will contract, but a

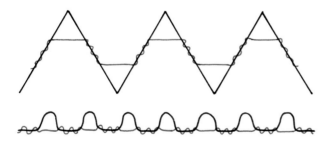

8.17—Top: See how the powerful floating active yarn (blue) pushes the fabric up and down into zigzag pleats. Bottom: The active yarns float only on one side of the fabric, and under only a few threads. This pushes the fabric up into small cords.

8.19—Weave draft for the checked fabric shown in figure 8.18.

8.20—Fabric with crepe yarn in both warp and weft, with one color for the warp and another for the weft. Squares of plain weave and floats are formed in both the warp and weft directions. The fabric is very elastic, almost like knitting.

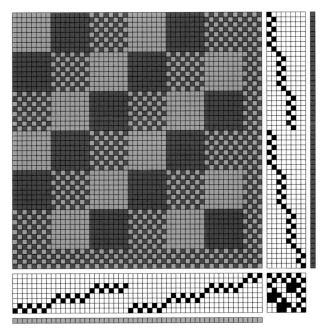

8.21—Weave draft for the crepe checks shown in figure 8.20.

sample will guide you, and from this you can make adjustments to your weave draft.

4. Double Weaves

Double weaving offers another exciting challenge for work with active yarns of all kinds, elastic, crepe and easily-fulled yarns. Double weaves have two layers which each have their own warp and weft and, if one uses an active yarn in one layer and a stable yarn in the other, this will create two entirely different cloth qualities. These two layers can be combined in endless ways, in lengthwise or crosswise stripes, in squares or with stitching points where the two cloths weave together. For many double weaves a minimum of 8 shafts is needed and, if there are patterns with more than two blocks, 12-16 shafts will be required. A computer-controlled loom gives more scope but, in this book, I will confine myself to describing set-ups for fewer shafts, so that they are accessible to everyone.

One of the more straightforward double weaves which is interesting to use in connection with active yarns is a simple structure with stripes of plain weave combined with "channels" of plain woven double cloth. One can, for example, use black on one side and white on the other, and a color-and-weave effect will then be produced in the tightly woven plain weave area. The draft given here does not include the possibility of the two layers exchanging places.

With an active yarn in the bottom layer and a stable yarn in the top layer, this structure can be used to produce a fabric that is smooth on the wrong side and has prominent ridges on the right side. The width of the raised stripes can be increased or decreased according to the yarn quality or sett that you are working with. In the plain weave stripes, where all the yarns weave together, the active yarn will be so tightly bound that these stripes will remain flat.

The same structure can be varied endlessly, for example with active yarns in the warp for both layers and for the whole of the weft. This will give one effect in the area where all yarns weave together and quite another in the double parts of the fabric. The sett will determine the effect that is produced -see the account given in the chapter on crepe

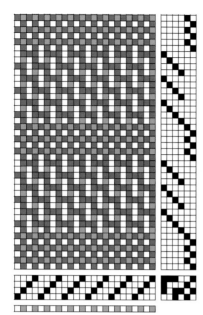

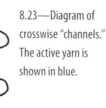

8.23—Diagram of crosswise "channels." The active yarn is shown in blue.

8.22—For crosswise "channels," 4 shafts and 6 treadles are needed. The stripes of plain weave and the "channels" can be treadled to the desired size.

yarns. Look through the photos in this book at the many different pictures of plain-woven fabrics in active yarns. Imagine a block of one of these effects, and then imagine a block woven with a smooth stable yarn.

Other double weaves result from the interchanging of the layers to form patterns. This is a structure that is very widely used. With an active yarn in one layer and a stable yarn in the other, an almost quilted appearance is obtained. A chequerboard effect can be produced, and this is shown in the chapter on shrinking yarns, where the structure is used with shrinking yarn in one layer and the polyester yarn Jet Tex in the other (figure 6.5). The fabric becomes

8.24—This fabric is a double weave on 4 shafts, with an open layer of black worsted/lycra in the lower layer and 11/1 lambswool on the top layer. The thread ratio of the bottom and top layers is 1:2. In the square areas the elastic thread weaves into the top layer, and in the areas that frame the squares, it floats under 12 threads. These floats create a raised edge. The areas where the two layers are joined together appear almost flat, and their size and form can be varied as desired. The fabric can be most easily woven, as shown on the draft, with the wrong side uppermost.

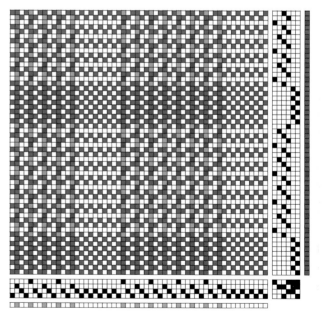

8.25—Weave draft of the orange fabric in double weave. The wrong side of the fabric is shown in figure 5.6.

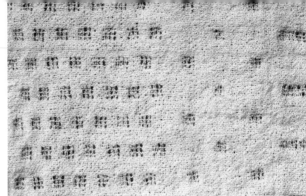

8.27—The front and back of a blue fabric, woven in a double weave with stitching points that bind the two layers together. The elastic yarn, in the lower layer, weaves into the upper layer, which consists of a stable yarn. The size of the ripples varies according to how closely one places the stitching points. (Note: In these illustrations the warp is running horizontally.)

like a tiny inflated airbed. There are many possibilities, such as varying the size of squares, producing color effects by weaving together blocks of plain weave and combining active and stable yarns. See, for example, Lise Frølund's neckpieces (figure 9.2) and Berthe Forchhammer's dress fabric (figure 9.6) and her computer woven wall hanging with dissolving yarn (figure 9.12).

Double weaves which have the two layers joined by stitching points, either scattered over the fabric or placed in tight rows, give other possibilities for textured textiles. With an active yarn in the lower layer and a relatively open sett, the fabric will contract strongly. The more stitching points there are in the structure, the greater will be the resistance to contraction and the size of the ripples will vary accordingly, as shown in figure 8.27.

8.26—30/1 wool crepe and 17/1 linen have been used to form the two layers of cloth in this sample. Many different colors have been used to create the blends and effects that occur when the fabric crepes. Later a selection of colors can be made from these.

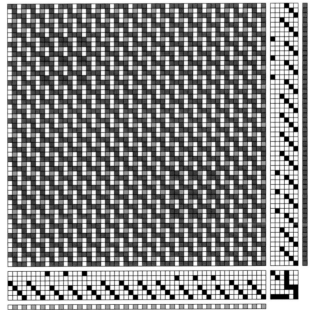

8.29—Weave draft for the double weave with stitching points.

Turquoise Summer Blouse with Cords in Linen and Wool

Warp: 11.3/1 lambswool, pale turquoise, and 17/1 linen in 4 different colors.

Weft: Linen/silk 42,000 m/kg in turquoise, and 30/1 wool crepe, 30,000 m/kg in natural white.

Sett: 30 epi (11.45 epcm), uneven denting in a 12 dent/inch reed (45/10 cm reed) (see chart).

Width at reed: 37 inches (97 cm), finished width 20 inches (53 cm).

Number of ends: 1104 + 4 selvedge ends.

Selvedge: Doubled threads for the first and last two heddles.

Weft sett: Linen/silk 18 ppi (7 ppcm) and wool crepe 26 ppi (10.5 ppcm).

Woven length: 2 pieces 37 inches (95 cm long).

Warp length: 2¾ yards (2.5 m), giving enough for a blouse and a small sample.

Weft sequence: 7 inches (17 cm) linen/silk in plain weave, 22 inches (55 cm) linen/silk and crepe wool, used according to the treadling draft, 7 inches (17 cm) linen/silk in plain weave. Two pieces are woven, one front and one back.

Weight of warp: Lambswool 3½ oz (100g) and linen 1 oz (27g) of each of the 4 colors.

Weight of weft: 1¼ oz (35g) linen/silk and ½ oz (14g) wool crepe.

Weave structure: Plain weave with floats. 4 shafts and 3 treadles.

Finishing and making-up:

The fabric should be washed in hot water with a little mild detergent. Give it two washes, as there is spinning oil in the lambswool.

The floating crepe wool threads cause the fabric to form narrow cords. A narrow rolled hem creates an attractive wavy edge at the armholes. The selvedges, consisting of 24 lambswool ends, should be turned to the wrong side and sewn in place with loose overcasting. The blouse is very simply constructed, with the two pieces sewn together on the shoulders. There is also a seam down one side, sewn just at the point where the cords begin, while the other side is simply knotted together. Alternatively, one could choose to sew up both the side seams.

▶Special tips for this set-up:

The part of the fabric forming the armholes is in plain weave, which gives a neat finish. The alternating stripes of linen and wool contract

Warp sequence:

Lambswool, turquoise	25		5		5		5		5	19
Linen, turquoise		9								
Linen, yellow-green				9						
Linen, blue-gray						9				
Linen, greenish								9		
					x 19					

Threading:

Lambswool	2	1			1	2	2			2	2	1			1	2	2				2
Linen		1	3	3	2			3	3	3			1	3	3	2			3	3	3	
	x 11					x 38															x 11

Above, beginning at left:

differently during finishing, the wool more than the linen, and this creates the seersucker effect.

If a slightly longer warp is set up, an extra piece can be woven, for example as a scarf or shawl.

8.33 – Here's a threading suggested for H shafts although only 3 are necessary.

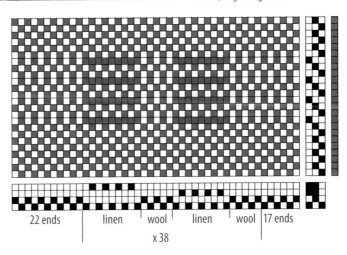

22 ends		linen	wool	linen	wool	17 ends
			x 38			

On Experimenting—Weaving Samples

There are many ways to be creative with yarns and weaving. One approach involves experimentation; others arise from the process of development, becoming inspired or weaving trial samples, depending upon the aim of the work. If you are one of those people who think it is completely absurd to get involved with these new yarns, which are often very fine and a little strange, then I refer you to Einstein, who is quoted as saying: "If an idea does not, at first, seem absurd, then there is no hope for it."

One thing I can promise you is that once you have experienced the many possibilities that are offered by working with active and stable yarns, and seen the exciting textiles that result after finishing, you will probably become just as fascinated and filled with curiosity as I have been. Sampling and experiment are exciting, and many new things can be discovered once you really involve yourself in this work. One "absurd" idea leads to another.

In this section I will describe my own experiences of experimenting with active yarns, and also draw on my many years as a teacher and practitioner within textiles.

I want the readers of this book to be seized with the desire to set to work with the new yarns that are now avail-

9.1—"A little something for the throat" was the weave assignment for the first year students at Kolding Design School in Spring 2007. Nina Cecilie Born took advantage of the double meaning in this assignment. When one has had "a little something for the throat," perhaps one may have had a little too much to drink, and therefore not be alert enough to drive, and so an accident and whiplash may follow. What is the throat in need of? Obviously a beautiful stiff collar that, in its beauty, far outstrips the boring, white expanded polystyrene version that the unfortunate person would otherwise be wearing! Nina has woven the collar—a piece of jewellery in my opinion—in plain weave and twill with a warp of Jet Tex and a weft of steel thread, nylon, bicycle inner tube and linen. This very creative approach to an assignment is typical of the way that students at the design school learn to work.

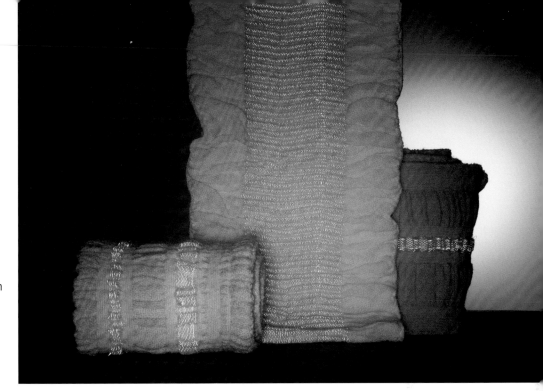

9.2—Lise Frølund is one of the Danish textile artists who quickly became fascinated by the new yarns with their special properties. Among other things, Lise Frølund has worked a great deal with light in her textiles. Here she has created items for practical use—neckpieces in double weave with wool and reflective yarn.

able, and to try fresh combinations and create new textiles. The Yarn Purchasing Association was started in 1998, on the initiative of a group of professional weavers and with support from the Danish Design Fund. The aim was to improve the basic resources for textile art and design and, as a result, the yarns became available to weavers at all levels.

This meant an improvement in weavers' access to new raw materials. The Yarn Purchasing Association of 1998 now imports a selection of yarns that are not otherwise available through the retail trade. The applies to classic yarns, as well as entirely new and untraditional yarns with various technical functions, and includes many of the yarns that are dealt with in this book. Some other specialist firms have since emerged. (See the list of suppliers.)

9.3—Detail of preparatory work for the textile decoration "Skimmer," woven by the Norwegian textile artist Jorun Schuman, who uses many of the new yarns available from The Yarn Purchasing Association. Here a synthetic yarn has been used that changes color according to its surroundings.

9.4 & 9.5—I do not often go around photographing things in my garden. But I do see a lot. And what is in my head is often also in my fingers. "Thinking with the fingers" is what I, as a weaver, do. "Thinking with the fingers" is also an expression for the kind of tacit knowledge that textile designer-craftsmen possess. I feel that it is important that we take responsibility for maintaining and passing on this tacit knowledge.

My own experiments generally take their starting point from my basic fascination with fibers, threads and colors -the shiny, the matt, the stiff, the soft -these all provide me with constant inspiration. I see textile textures everywhere, and I have weaving in mind the whole time; it is so strong a feeling that it is a large part of my identity.

I was trained as a weaver with an old fashioned apprenticeship, a craft training with practical experience and routine, never to be forgotten. During my training with Anette Juel and later with Ann-Mari Kornerup, I learned a lot, including the weaving of samples. Along with this came perseverance, so that working towards a goal, sticking with it, unpicking and repeating until the goal was reached, came to seem the most natural thing in the world! I am glad of the solid grounding that I gained in that way.

It was craft skill, combined with a feeling for, and knowledge of, materials, that really provided the springboard for me when I began to weave samples, to develop and research—yes, to experiment. I started trying out the new active crepe yarns in 1998 and, once I had achieved an effect that I was pleased with and that others also appreciated, I set to work on the small-scale production of scarves and shawls. Throughout my time as a weaver, I have always enjoyed being at the loom. The varied work, moving between making samples, sketches and plans, sorting out rejects and making new samples, going back to the loom to weave again, and so on, has given me peace in body and mind and has always suited me very well.

9.7—TITBIT model in a pleated fabric in wool crepe and linen. The density of the pleats varies in this fabric. The blouse is designed and made by Elisabeth Hagen. The fabric is woven in plain weave and is one of those in which I have endlessly varied the color combinations. Every time I try a new color, intending just to weave a couple of stripes in the starting border, something happens! I am seized by the possibilities of seeing that color together with other colors, and suddenly I find I have woven 2 yards.

9.6—Berthe Forchhammer produced a double-woven length in wool crepe for the Guild of Printers and Weavers exhibition "Stripes," shown at the Round Tower, Copenhagen in 2006. The crepe yarns were S-spun and Z-spun in both warp and weft. Shown here is a section of a dress in the same fabric, which Berthe contributed to the Biennalen for Kunsthåndværk [Art and Design] in 2007.

In this way, many happy accidents have directed the path that my career has taken.

The Continuing Experiment

Among the weavers who have inspired me is Anni Albers, from the German Bauhaus, which had great significance for the development of textile art and design in Denmark. She is quoted as saying:

"The material itself is full of suggestions for its use if we approach it unaggressively, receptively."

As a weaver, I have had the opportunity to develop this receptive approach in an inspiring collaboration with the dress designer Elisabeth Hagen. Together we have created the collection TITBIT, which received an award for innovation, from Statens Kunstfond [The State Fund for Art in Denmark] in 2005. My first meeting with Elisabeth was itself something of an accident.

Teaching has been a large part of my life in textiles. I really enjoy communicating my own pleasure in the subject, sharing it and seeing others become fascinated with the possibilities or simply the craft. It was in just such a teaching situation that I came to know Elisabeth Hagen and her

special skills. Elisabeth is a clothing designer and in 2002 we began to collaborate on a collection of one-off garments, which we gave the name TITBIT.

Elisabeth experimented first with a fabric of mine that was actually woven for shawls. Elisabeth shapes and cuts directly on the dressmaker's dummy, a method that allows her to exploit my fabrics with active yarns, in an optimum and unique way. The development of the TITBIT collection is an ongoing game of ping-pong between us. I constantly vary the texture, contraction, color etc, in my fabrics, and this stimulates Elisabeth to create new one-off blouses that, in turn, lead me to use the active yarns in new ways.

The blouse fabric in linen and ramie (figure 9.8) has been developed from a cloth quality intended for scarves, similar to that shown in figure 7.1.

I was interested to see how they contracted during finishing. Elisabeth later looked at this fabric, with the idea of designing some light summer blouses. I had cut off some of the fabric, partway through weaving the 22 yards (20 m) length, and so there was a 4 inch (10 cm) length of preparatory weaving and a small area of unwoven warp, where a stick had been laid in the warp. Two days later when I saw how Elisabeth had draped the fabric on the dummy, I discovered that she had used the preparatory weaving to form the neckline and that the unwoven warp threads formed a very special and delicate effect at the edge. It looked enchanting. Because of the overspun linen, the unwoven area curled up almost like a little piece of lace but, unfortunately, some of the linen threads tended to slip out into this open area. I rushed home and experimented with ways to get the threads to stay in place so that the open effect would not be spoiled. After a couple of attempts, I found that ⅜ inch (a centimeter) of very fine crepe threads would

9.8—This blouse is woven with a linen/ramie hard-spun crepe yarn, which is responsible for the texture of the fabric. It is a TITBIT model from 2004 and the story behind its creation demonstrates one of the ways in which experiments—at least for me—can be open and without preconceptions. The warp consisted of different qualities and colors of linen in small stripes, including some crepe yarn.

9.10—Here a scalloped edge has been produced, where narrow stripes of an active crepe yarn are woven between broader linen stripes. The warp consists of a crepe yarn in the areas where the fabric is pleating, while a stable yarn has been used for the smooth areas that form the scalloped edge. Note: In this illustration the warp runs horizontally and the weft vertically.

prevent the slippage. Later this idea was used for the whole of the back of the blouse so that the open texture became a part of the overall effect (figure 9.8).

Here is some advice and some simple instructions about how to get started with making samples and experimenting with active and stable yarns.

Use the properties of the active yarns

Test the energy of the yarn by washing a small skein. Look carefully at the threads, stretch them and notice how much power of contraction the yarn has. Take note of the size of the curls and any hairiness.

Set up a warp with a stable yarn—preferably a fine one. Tie up the loom for plain weave and 2/2 or 1/3 twill. Weave samples of about 4 inches (10 cm), with different crepe yarns, and using an open weft sett. Then repeat, doubling the sett of the weft. Also try an elastic yarn. Cut off the samples and wash them. Look at the results and select those you think most exciting, and then try alternating stripes of active and stable yarns. Experiment more widely, trying different structures. Keep on looking at the finished samples to choose the next combination, so you are building on your experience.

Rethread the warp at a different sett and see what happens. Try pulling some threads out of the reed so that you have a very open sett. Try varying the density across the warp.

Try setting up the active yarn as a warp and make samples in the same way. Weave with stable yarns. Then weave with active yarns, so you have crepe yarns crossing one another, and something entirely different will happen.

Think about the contrasts in the "personalities" of the yarns. Shiny–matt. Hard–soft. Thick–thin.

Use the properties of the structures

Weave structures with many intersection points do not need so many ends/inch or cm to create texture. Structures with many floats, when used with active yarns, give powerful contractions.

Make a plain weave draft—on WeavePoint if you like—and then draw in different floats. Arrange them so that the structure suits the number of shafts you have on your loom. Do the same with other weave structures. Have a look at the chapter on suitable weaves, try some of these structures and see what happens. Think about your own loom and the possibilities that are offered by its number of shafts. Do not be afraid to try several new tie-ups during the course of one sample.

Look at the colors

If you are lucky and have many skeins and balls of yarn in

9.11 — Mette Kaa produced plissé woven in twill with warp-and-weft effect for black and white dresses for the guild of printers and weavers 60th anniversary exhibition "Stripes," shown at the Round Tower in 2006. The pleats were made by weaving in additional threads to pull the pleats into position and then it was washed, dried and shrunk. The warp is worsted yarn and the weft size 60,000 monofilament and Corneta MX Transparent.

different colors, then lay these out on the table so you can see them together; move them round and take away those you do not think you will use on this occasion. It does not matter that these are different yarn qualities. When you are satisfied with the colors, you can make color windings on pieces of card or simply take a few strands of each color and twist them together to see how they blend.

If your own stock is not very large, then exchange yarns with your weaving friends. Just a single spool can allow you to see how that color works with the others. It is good to see the colors in textile materials. For me it feels different from even the most beautiful watercolor. Both forms of visualization are worth using. One can easily change a stripe in the warp by arranging beforehand to have threads available in two different colors. First try one color, then pull that thread out of the reed and heddle and put in the new color.

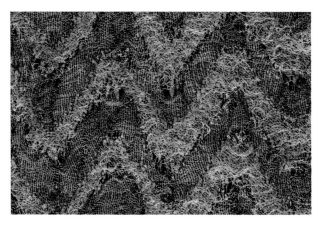

9.12—Section of "Transformation," a wall decoration woven by Berthe Forchhammer in collaboration with Malene Pawlas in 2003. It is woven on a computer-controlled loom with 24 shafts with an intermittent draft and double woven blocks. One of the weft yarns is dissolvable and is washed out after weaving, leaving areas of unwoven warp threads.

Think about the use of the textile

Should it be easily formed and drape smoothly? Have a firm handle or a heavy drape? Should it shine and be glossy? Are you aiming for coziness or beauty? Find yarns that match your wishes. Make a test sample—this does not need to be very large to give you a feeling for the sett etc. Follow this up with a proper weave sample and remember to make this large. Active yarns contract and so the sample may finish up perhaps half the size. The more you weave samples and study the effects, the better you will become at making the next choice.

Or, do not think about the use at all

Let the colors guide you. Let your curiosity about a particular weave structure guide you. Talk with your fellow weavers, if there are any. Or talk with yourself, arguing back and forth, then relax for while. Look at it again in the morning.

All creative work is a dialogue between the person and the materials.

There is an interplay between the types of yarn that have been chosen and the way in which they are woven, which is unbelievably exciting. All the time, I am discovering new possibilities by changing the sett, the weave or the type of yarn. Gradually, as one gets to know the active yarns, it becomes easier to control the process. In each new set-up, something new will turn up, which leads on to the next weave sample. The continuing experiment—the endless fascination.

I hope that I have given you the courage to set to work on developing designs, especially with active yarns. All my advice takes its starting point from the way in which I work myself, but this is also the approach that I have found to be successful in inspiring and motivating the many participants in my courses, in various weaving groups around the country. This motivation goes beyond simply using other people's recipes and ideas. As the weaver Gina Hedegaard—President of Danish Society of Designer-Craftsmen -once said:

"That's just for absolute beginners. It is much more fun to find your own means of expression."

At present, most education in woven textiles has little to do with the routine of actually weaving. Priorities are very different. Some things have been lost, as other concerns have come to the fore. Designing with computers and digital thread-controlled looms is an exciting development, which offers new possibilities for those professionally involved in textiles. But a firm grounding in craftsmanship and knowledge of materials provide a good starting point for experiments on the loom. Many people who weave in their spare time are working towards, and achieving, that freedom, which is such an essential part of my own personal work in weaving.

9.13—Ann Richards—the English textile artist—has worked intensively with active yarns for many years. Ann Richards was educated as a biologist and is fascinated by the wing construction of butterflies and other insects. She works in a very refined way with yarns that include silk crepe, silk/steel and paper. She forms these into fantastic neckpieces, which have been exhibited, among other places, at the Danish Museum of Art and Design in Copenhagen in 2006.

I am certain that many exciting yarns will come on to the market in the coming years, both in Denmark and abroad, yarns in all sorts of fibers, both natural and synthetic. These "magical" materials will offer us new possibilities.

I hope all the explanations and tips in this book can help you in your first attempts with the new active and magical yarns. Perhaps you will find other ways of handling these lively yarns, to suit your hands and your loom. There are many ways of setting up looms and craft traditions vary from one country to another. Use the experience that you already have as the basis for picking up fresh skills with the new "magical" yarns —and enjoy them.

To be a weaver is to be a "look and touch" person.

Finishing Active Yarns

I am still intensely fascinated by weaving flat pieces of cloth, using active yarns, on my faithful companion— the traditional shaft loom. To begin with, I was completely astonished by the effects that were simply "given" to me by the materials, when the weaving was cut from the loom and put into hot water. Out of the water came a wavy, or pleated or bubbly piece of cloth—a piece of fabric that had a life of its own.

When textiles made with active yarns are completed and cut from the loom, most of them will be entirely smooth and it can seem impossible that they should become bubbly, pleated or creped pieces of cloth. But it is here that the "magical" experience occurs. The active yarns contract in the finishing and, depending on the amount of active yarn, the sett and weave structure, the fabric will draw itself together to form a textured textile. This really gives an "aha experience," where everyone on my courses gathers together to say: "no!" and "oh!" and "ah!" and "look at that…"

Finishing is very much the same for most active yarns. Weavings with crepe yarns (overspun) or elastic yarns (with lycra) should be placed in hot water at approximately 140° F/60° C. Always check the instructions about temperature, for each particular yarn, with your supplier. It is necessary to wear rubber gloves, or you will burn your fingers.

The hot water will release the steam setting, which the yarn has been given during production to make it easier to work with. Take care that all the yarn and fibers have taken up the hot water, and squeeze the fabric to help it form the bubbles, pleats or waves that you have planned. Fabrics with overspun yarns should be allowed to lie in the water for a while to ensure that all the steam setting has been released. Silk crepe yarns take longer to absorb the hot water and it can be helpful to put a little liquid soap into

10.1—Before finishing the fabric is entirely flat. The warp stripes alternate between linen size 26 and 30/1 wool crepe, producing two different effects: tight pleats, where there is crepe yarn, and ripples, where there is linen.

the water. Fabrics with elastic yarns contract quickly, with lightening speed. After the water has been pressed out of the fabric, for example with a hand-towel, the fabric is carefully smoothed out, pulled lengthwise in the direction of any pleats and placed in the desired shape, then laid flat to dry.

Never let the fabric dry hanging or stretched. With my production work for TITBIT, where the warp is entirely crepe yarn, I roll the fabrics in a hand-towel, which helps to position the pleats, before I lay the pieces out to dry.

After finishing, the woven fabric will be elastic and will have become smaller, especially if it has a structure where the crepe yarns form floats. If the textile loses its elasticity and becomes stretched in use, which tends to happen particularly with crepe yarns, then it will contract once again if it is placed in hot water and laid out to dry, in the same way as when it was first finished.

10.2—This fabric has been woven with two-ply lambswool in the warp and singles lambswool in the weft. The small bobbles appear when the fabric is felted in a washing machine. A purple thread is woven to form long floats, which are cut before finishing, and which felt together to form the small bobbles.

Fulling

All finishing that involves fulling requires some testing if you are to be entirely certain of the result.

The process of fulling has been widely used for hand-woven cloth, especially for blankets before brushing to raise the surface. The fabric is put into water at 104° F/ 40° C together with soapflakes, which are first dissolved in boiling water. The fabric is thoroughly pressed together in the soapy water, the length and vigour of this treatment depending on how easily the wool felts and the result that is required. One can, of course, use a washing machine for fulling.

Lambswool yarns, which I have used for the sample with small bobbles (figure 10.2), tolerate machine full-ing very well. I have given the fabric a normal color wash at 104° F/40° C. But there are large differences between washing machines, so here you must really feel your way. If you want to test how a fabric will full in the wash-ing machine, using just a small sample, then put in some dishcloths or something similar, to give the effect of a full length of fabric in the machine. If the small sample were put in alone, it would become much too heavily finished.

Fulling by hand works very well with materials that full easily, since it has the advantage that you can feel the fabric throughout the process and judge how much it is felting together. For example, hand fulling was used to finish the fabric for the little black jacket woven by Irene Madsen from Merino wool and silver colored Corneta TM (figure 6.6).

Another method of fulling is to use a tumble dryer, and

this is especially suitable for the Merino yarns, which full very readily. The fabric should be wet, so make sure that all the wool has absorbed the water, then lay the fabric in the tumble dryer with a warm air setting. It is possible to check on the fabric throughout the process, and stop when it has reached the desired quality. Fulling is more effective if the fabric is first rinsed thoroughly with soapy water. After this, lay the wet, soapy fabric in a large plastic bag, close it up and allow the whole bag to roll around in the tumble dryer. You can read more about many of these methods of fulling in books on felting.

Explanatory guidelines about yarns, setts and percentages of shrinkage can be seen in the shrinkage chart and in the list of yarns and suppliers. There are also references to the weave structure diagrams and illustrations used in the book.

Be aware that the percentage of shrinkage can vary according to the energy of the different yarns. For example, figure 3.2 clearly shows the large variations in the contracting power of different crepe yarns. Similarly, the slightest variation in sett can have great importance.

Hopefully, the charts will be helpful in your first experiments on the loom.

Sewing and Making up

Fabrics that are textured, pleated etc. are not always easy to sew. It requires a little practice and some tests on a sample to find out which hem will give the best result on a particular piece of cloth.

I always sew the edges on my pleated scarves, as well as many other scarves with active yarns, before wet finishing. It is simply easier. For example, I advise you to zigzag along the edge of the fabric as soon as you have cut a clean edge. Then make a narrow rolled hem, preferably using a machine stitch that gives two straight stitches, followed by a zigzag stitch.

If your sewing machine does not have this type of stitch, then use a normal zigzag instead. The hem will flare a little and form a nice wavy edge, which can clearly be seen, for example, in the silver and black scarf project, in the chapter on metal yarns (figure 4.8).

Sewing clothing is more demanding. Here it is necessary to finish the fabric first to get a feeling for its size and elasticity. It is not possible simply to lay a dress pattern on it. I suggest that you try draping the fabric around a dressmaker's dummy to see how it behaves. If you do not have a dummy, then you need a friend or family member to act as a model.

Shrinkage Chart

The chart is intended as a practical tool. However, the information and references are given with the reservation that there may be mistakes and inaccuracies. The figure numbers refer to the illustrations in the book.

Warp	Weft	Weave	Epcm shrinkage	Ppcm weftwise	Approx. shrinkage	Approx. warpwise	Figure
Singles wool	30/1 Wool crepe	Plain weave	8	6	30%	Normal	3.15
Singles wool	30/1 Wool crepe	Plain weave	8	12	50%	Normal	3.15
Singles wool	Singles wool Wool crepe, alternating 2 S, 2 Z	Plain weave	8	8	45%	Normal	
30/1 Wool crepe	26/1 Linen	Plain weave	12	12	4%	50%	3.5
30/1 Wool crepe	30/1 Wool crepe	Plain weave	12	12	50%	50%	1.2
Linen: 6 ends, linen/ramie: 1 end, 28/2 Merino, easy felting: 1 end	16/1 Linen	2/2 twill	8	6	Normal	18%	3.9
28/2 Merino wool	60/2 Silk, with 30/1 wool crepe for floats	Plain weave with floats, draft 8.15, treadling 1	9	10 wool crepe:2, silk: 2	60%	Normal	3.18
Stripes with 8 ends 17/1 linen and 8 ends 30/1 Wool crepe	Stripes with 8 ends linen 17/1 and 8 ends 30/1 Wool crepe	2/2 twill	8 ends	8 ends	36%	40-50%	8.31
Corneta MX Transparent	30/1 Wool crepe	Plain weave	12 ends	12 ends	64%	Usually disappears	4.8
Corneta MX Transparent	30/1 Wool crepe with stripes of Jet Tex	Plain weave, cuffs	12 ends	Wool crepe 12 ends Jet Tex 11 ends	20%	Usually disappears	4.5
11/1 Lambswool and worsted with lycra	11/1 Lambswool and worsted yarn with lycra	Plain weave with blocks in double weave, draft 8.25	9 ends	9 ends	35-40%	35-40%	8.24
11/1 Lambswool	11/1 Lambswool and worsted yarn with lycra	Double weave with floats, draft 5.9	6 ends	12 ends	35%	20%	5.7 and 5.8
Jet Tex and wool/acrylic woolen yarn	Jet Tex and wool/acrylic woolen yarn	Double weave, bound at pattern change	16 ends, 8 in each layer	16 ends, 8 in each layer	25%	25%	6.5
4 ends 28/2 Merino wool and 1 double end linen with lycra	6 ends 60/2 Silk and 1 double spooled wool crepe	Plain weave with floats, draft 8.8	12 ends	8 ends	Usually disappears	50%	8.7
12 ends 28/2 Merino wool and 5 ends 30/1 Wool crepe	12 ends 28/2 Merino wool and 5 ends 30/1 wool crepe	Plain weave with floats, draft 8.19	10 ends	10 ends	35-40%	35-40%	8.18
30/1 Wool crepe	30/1 Wool crepe	Plain weave with floats draft 8.21	10 double ends	10 double ends	50%	50%	8.20
11/1 Lambswool and linen/lycra	11/1 Lambswool and linen/ lycra	Double weave with stitching points. Draft 8.29	12 ends, 6 wool and 6 linen/lycra	12 ends, 6 wool and 6 linen/lycra	45%	45%	8.27 and 8.28
9 ends linen 17/1 and 5 ends 11/1 Lambswool	42/2 Silk/linen and 30/1 wool crepe	Plain weave with floats, draft 8.33	11.5 ends	10.5 ends	45%	Usually disappears	8.31 and 8.33

Yarns and Suppliers

Yarns	Yarn Size	Ply Twist Direction	Fiber	M/kg	Tpm	Finishing	Characteristics	Suppliers
Japanese wool crepe yarn	30	S and Z	100% worsted wool	30,000	1000	140° F/60° C		YPA+ Væv and Flet
Worsted yarn with lycra	36/2		98% wool, 2 % lycra	18,000		104° F/40° C	Elastic	YPA
Demeter Merino wool	28/2		100% worsted Merino wool	14,000			Easily fulled, biodynamic	YPA
Demeter Merino wool	48/2		100% worsted Merinowool	24,000			Easily fulled, biodynamic	YPA
Scottish lambswool	11,3/1		100% lambswool	11,300			Yarn contains spinning oils and will soften after washing.	Væv and Flet
Superwash wool	30/2		100% Merino wool	15,000			Superwash treated wool *does not* full.	YPA
Wool crepe with dissolvable core	14/1		72% wool, 8% polyamid, 20% polyvinyl-alcohol	14,000	480	140° F/60° C	The yarn gets a softer handle when the inner core is dissolved so that air enters the yarn and it softens.	YPA
Woolen wool/acrylic yarn	40/2		60% wool, 40% acrylic	20,000		175° F/80° C	The yarn felts and becomes thicker and changes from a 40/2 to a 26/2 count after finishing	YPA
2-ply Wool crepe	52/2		100% wool	26,000	1180	Warm water		Væv and Flet
Linen with lycra	27			27,000		Warm water	Elastic	YPA
Linen/ramie crepe yarn	15/1		30% linen, 70% ramie	15,000	760	140° F/60° C		YPA
Kateku single linen	26/1		100% linen	26,000				Not available
Lithuania single linen	17/1		100% linen	17,000				Væv and Flet
Tormalina single linen	14/1		100% linen	14,000				YPA
1-ply Linen	16/1		100% linen	11,000				Available at most weaving suppliers
Linen/silk			Linen/silk	42,000				Væv and Flet
Silk crepe	34	S	100% silk	34,000		Warm water		YPA
Silk and lycra	70/1		Schappesilk with lycra	70,000		Warm water	Elastic	YPA
Silk and steel, stretch silk	82/2		65 % silk, 35 % stainless steel	41,000			Preserves the folds and creases in the elastic	YPA
Silk crepe	4x40/44 denier	S and Z	100% silk	53,570		Warm water	The yarn must be degummed: boil for 1 hour in soapy water and rinse well	Væv and Flet
Cotton and lycra	34/2		Mercerized cotton with lycra	14,500		Warm water	Cotton and lycra threads are very loosely plied	Væv and Flet, Karen Noe
Cotton crepe	50/1	Z	100% cotton	50,000	1450	140° F/60° C	Creping in warm water	YPA

Yarns	Yarn Size	Ply Twist Direction	Fiber	M/kg	Tpm	Finishing	Characteristics	Suppliers
Merc. cotton	34/2		100% cotton	17,000				Karen Noe, sells fine mercerizes cotton yarns
Elastane	19		100% poly-urethane				Very elastic, semi-transparent	YPA
Corneta MX Transparent	86/1		64% polyester, 38% polyamid	86,000			Tolerates fine wash cycle and ironing on low temperature	YPA
Corneta TM	30		Black viscose with polyesterfilm	30,000			Tolerates fine wash cycle and ironing on low temperature	Væv and Flet
Jet Tex	Dtex 600		100% polyester	16,600				YPA
Reflekta	16		91% polyester, 9% polyacrylic	16,000			Polyester foil yarn with gray reflective material added	YPA
Copper thread	30		85% copper, 15% polyamid	30,000			Preserves the folds and creases in the fabric	YPA
Gold thread	50/1		75 % gold covered silver, 25 % silk	50,000				YPA
Silver thread	50/1		75 % silver, 25 % silk	50,000				YPA
Double stainless steel yarn	4/2	Z	100 % steel	2,000				YPA

YPA= Yarn Purchasing Association of 1998

USA:
Habu Textiles
135 West 29th Street, Suite 804
New York, NY 10001
habu@habutextiles.com
www.habutextiles.com

Denmark:
BC Garn
Albuen 56A, 6000 Kolding
Tel: 75 89 73 84
www.garn.dk

Yarn Purchasing Association of 1998
(Must be a member)
Henv.: Berthe Forchhammer
Tel: 20 74 52 47
berthe.forchhammer@gmail.com
www.yarn.dk

Væv & Flet
Nordrupvej 58, 4100 Ringsted
Tel: 57 64 05 00/20 72 28 35
mail@vaevandflet.dk
www.vaevandflet.dk

Karen Noe Design
Søndergade 23, 7171 Woolum
Tel: 75 67 97 33
www..karen-noe.dk

Sweden:
Ehaus Textil & Konsthantverk
Shop and studio
Edavägen 9, 360 52 Kosta
Tel: + 46 0478-508 08
info@ehaustextil.se
www.ehaustextil.se

England:
Fibercrafts
Old Portsmouth Road, Peasmarsh
GUILDFORD, Surrey GU3 1LZ
sales@fibercrafts.com
www.fibercrafts.com

The Handweavers Studio
29 Haroldstone Road
London, E17 7AN
handweaversstudio@msn.com
www.handweaversstudio.co.uk

Glossary

Cone. A conical shaped form on which many types of yarn are wound.

Cords are rather small pleats that, in principle, could be produced by sewing. In this book, the term is used particularly to refer to small raised ridges, which are produced through the floating of an active yarn.

Creping is the reaction that takes place when a fabric draws together because of the weave structure and/or the use of an active yarn.

Crepon. A classic fabric type woven with a passive warp and an overspun weft.

Double weaves are structures in which there are two or more warps and/or wefts. These can form two or more layers or be woven together to give different weave structures, colors or qualities on the two sides.

Drafting is the process of recording raised and lowered threads, together with threading, treadling and treadle tie-up.

Felting occurs when wool fibers bind together, due to agitation in hot soapy water. Wool fibers have small barbs, or scales, which catch on one another so that the fibers cannot be separated. Under the microscope, the surface of the wool fiber resembles that of a pine cone.

Felting properties. The ability of the fiber or the yarn to felt during finishing.

Floating selvedge. An end that has not been threaded through a heddle, at the edge of the warp. This thread does not rise or fall during treadling, but stays in the middle of the shed. As the shuttle is placed in the shed, it passes over a floating selvedge thread on one side, and emerges underneath the floating selvedge thread on the other side. In this way the weft thread is bound into the weave with every pick. This is used for structures where the selvedge threads would otherwise not bind in for long distances.

Floats occur where warp or weft threads do not interlace with the cloth but, instead, lie loose on the front or back of the fabric.

Foil yarn is composed of 1 mm wide strips cut from a synthetic material.

Intersection. The point where threads cross over one another or pass from one side of the cloth to the other. Plain weave has the largest number of intersection points.

Kinks are small crinkles that appear in a thread that has been given too many twists for it to remain smooth.

Lycra is an elastic fiber made from elastane.

Making a cross is the process of crossing warp threads, to separate them, while making the warp. If several threads are used together to make the warp, the cross can be made with the fingers, as described in this book, or using a paddle. (see chapter on practical instructions).

Monofilament is a yarn formed of a single continuous synthetic fiber.

Niddy-noddy. A tool used for winding yarn into hanks (skeins), for example, after spinning.

Plain weave is the simplest weave structure. Threads interlace over-one-under one.

Pleats are lengthwise ridges or sharp folds, which develop through the use of many of the magical materials. They can also be produced through heat treatment or pressing.

Polyamide thread/yarn is made of the synthetic material polyamide (nylon).

Polyvinyl alcohol is a soluble fiber which dissolves in water.

Ramie is a vegetable fiber, derived from the stem of the Chinese nettle. It is prepared in the same way as flax. It is a very smooth, long fiber and is sometimes called "false silk."

Reel. A tool for winding yarn into hanks (skeins) after spinning or from a cone Skeins are required if the yarn is to be washed or dyed.

Reeling is the process of winding yarn on to a reel or similar tool.

Sizing the warp. Used to strengthen a delicate warp. It is the painting, dipping or spraying of the warp using a gluey substance which, when dry, will stiffen and strengthen the threads. After weaving it is removed by washing. Boiled flax seeds were formerly used to make size and this works well, but spray starch is easier to work with. Alternatively one can use manutex, which is a paste used in fabric printing.

Skip. The same as a float. The word is often used to indicate a thread that accidentally passes over several threads when it should have woven in.

Skip draft. A system of threading used for closely set and delicate warps so that they do not suffer too much wear during weaving.

S-spun yarn is twisted counterclockwise.

Straight draft. A threading arrangement where the heddles are threaded on shafts 1, 2, 3 and 4 in sequence (or on a larger number of shafts in sequence).

Superwash wool has been treated so that it does not felt when agitated in hot water.

Tpm is an abbreviation of "turns per meter" and refers to the amount of twists in a yarn (see Yarn twist).

Undercoat wool. Wool fiber from the undercoat of sheep or other animals. The undercoat has especially fine, soft fibers and good felting properties.

Warp. The threads that run lengthwise in the cloth.

Weave draft. A schematic drawing of the way that threads cross one another (or interlace) in a woven piece of cloth.

Weave notation or drafting is the recording of raised and lowered threads in a weave draft.

WeavePoint is a computer weave drafting program. Available in different versions, see: www.weavepoint.com.

Weft. The threads that run across the width of the cloth.

Yarn count. There are several different systems. In this book all the yarn counts are given in the metric system. The first figure gives the number of kilometers/kg. The second specifies the number of threads that make up the yarn. For example: 7/2 is a 2-ply yarn. Each of the single threads that compose it run to 7,000 m/kg, so that the plied yarn runs to half this amount, i.e. 3,500 m/kg. Usually, the twisting together of the threads makes the length a little shorter, so that it will often be only 3,300 bm/kg. 17/1 indicates a yarn composed of a single thread which runs to 17,000 m/kg.

Yarn twist. The numbers of turns/meter in a yarn (tpm).

Z-spun yarn is twisted in a clockwise direction.

Further Reading

Adam, Paulette, Mai-Britt Bille, Lisbeth Degn
og Lisbeth Tolstrup:
Weaving for Venus: A Textbook
Hovedland 2006. (Kunst og håndværk)
ISBN: 87-7739-841-6

Albers, Anni:
On Weaving
Dover Publications 2003 (1965)
ISBN 0486431924

Arn-Grischott, Ursina:
Double Weaving for the Hand Weaver:
A Handbook for Double and Multi-Layer Weaving
Haupt 1997
ISBN: 3258056064

Droste, M. og Manfred Ludewig (red.):
Bauhaus Weaving
G+H Verlag, Berlin 1998
ISBN 3-931768-20-1

Eriksson, Mariana, Gunnel Gustavsson,
Kerstin Lovallius:
Warp and Weft: Lessons in Drafting
for Handweaving
Trafalgar Square Books, 2011
ISBN: 978-1-57076-473-8

Ignell, Tina:
Sculptural Textiles and Sacred Weavings
I Vävmagasinet 2006, nr. 4,
side 6-9

Lund-Iversen, Berit:
Weaving: Lessons in Drafting
2. utgave. Universitetsforlaget 1981 (1980).
ISBN: 82-00-28183-3

Paulli Andersen, M. K.:
Weaving Book
Borgen 1981 (1971).
ISBN: 87-418-2682-5

Rasmussen, Inger Johanne:
Weaving Book: Textiles and Equipment
Tell 2001.
ISBN: 82-7522-140-4

Sutton, Ann:
The Structure of Weaving
B.T. Batsford 1986 (1982).
ISBN 0713454911

Sutton, Ann and Diana Sheehan:
Ideas in Weaving
B.T. Batsford 1989.
ISBN: 0713461519